THE WILL TO
WIN

Published by CelebrityPress®, Orlando, FL.

CelebrityPress® is a registered trademark.

Printed in the United States of America.

ISBN: 978-1-7322843-1-9
LCCN: 2018945986

Most CelebrityPress® titles are available at special quantity discounts for bulk purchases for sales promotions, premiums, fundraising, and educational use. Special versions or book excerpts can also be created to fit specific needs.

For more information, please write:
CelebrityPress®
520 N. Orlando Ave, #2
Winter Park, FL 32789
or call 1.877.261.4930

Visit us online at: www.CelebrityPressPublishing.com

THE WILL TO WIN

CelebrityPress®
Winter Park, Florida

CONTENTS

CHAPTER 1

DO SOMETHING EVERY DAY

BY BRIAN TRACY

"My success evolved from working hard at the business at hand every day."
~ Johnny Carson

Many studies have been conducted over the years to try to determine why some people are more successful than others.

Hundreds, even thousands of salespeople, staff and managers have been interviewed, tested and studied in an attempt to identify the common denominators of success. One of the most important success factors discovered, over and over again, is the quality of "Action Orientation."

Successful people are *intensely* action oriented. They seem to move faster than unsuccessful people. They are busier. They try more things, and they try harder. They start a little earlier and they stay a little later.

They are in constant motion.

Unsuccessful people, on the other hand, start at the last moment necessary and quit at the first moment possible. They are fastidious about taking every minute of coffee breaks, lunch hours, sick leave and vacations. They sometimes brag, "When I am not at work, I never even think about it."

A STORY OF FAILURE

We used to have an employee who was always late. When we spoke to him about this, he explained that his reason for being late was the traffic.

We suggested to him that he leave earlier so that the traffic would not be a problem. He was shocked. He said, "But if I left earlier, and there was no traffic, I might arrive at work earlier than my starting time. I couldn't possibly do that!"

Needless to say, we soon let him go and hired someone else with a greater sense of responsibility and commitment. We heard later that he has continued on with the endless round of part-time jobs and unemployment that has marked his career throughout his life.

His attitude has set him up for failure time and time again.

THE LAW OF COMPENSATION

In his famous essay *Compensation*, Ralph Waldo Emerson wrote:

"You will always be compensated in life in direct proportion to the value of your contribution."

If you want to increase the size of your rewards, you must increase the quality and quantity of your results. If you want to get more out, you have to put more in. And there is no other way.

Napoleon Hill found that the key quality of successful men and women, most of whom started at the bottom, many of them penniless, was that early in life, they developed the habit of "going the extra mile."

They discovered, as the old saying goes, that "There are never any traffic jams on the extra mile."

THE QUALITY OF SELF-MADE MILLIONAIRES

In one study of self-made millionaires, researchers interviewed thousands of men and women who had started with nothing and who had accumulated more than a million dollars in the course of their careers.

These self-made millionaires almost unanimously agreed that their success was the result of always "doing more than they were paid for." They had made it a habit from their first jobs to always put in more than they took out.

They were always looking for ways to contribute beyond what was expected of them.

LIFE LONG CAREER SUCCESS

When I speak to a graduating class of business students, they often ask me, usually with some concern, if I can give them some suggestions or ideas on what they can do to be successful in the world of work.

I always give them the same advice. It worked for me when I was a young man and it works for everybody, at every stage of his or her career. My advice consists of two parts.

First, as soon as you get settled in at your new job, and you are on top of your work, go to your boss and tell him or her that you want "more responsibility." Tell him or her that you are determined to make the maximum contribution possible in this organization, and that you would very much like "more responsibility" whenever it becomes available.

When I first started doing this as a young executive with a large corporation, my boss nodded and smiled and thanked me for my interest. But nothing happened, at least for a while.

Every few days, I would report to my boss and mention, in part, that I wanted "more responsibility."

YOUR CHANCE WILL COME

After a few weeks of this, my boss gave me a project to study and evaluate.

I jumped on it like a dog jumping on a bone and ran off. I worked day and night, and throughout the weekend, tearing that project apart, gathering research, reassembling the details and putting together a report and a proposal.

On Monday morning, I was back to my boss with a complete proposal on the project. He was obviously surprised. He said, "There was no rush. I didn't expect anything back from you for a week or two."

I thanked him for his concern and told him that, "This project evaluation is complete, as you requested. And by the way, I would really like more responsibility."

Things began to change for me very soon after that project evaluation. A week later, I was given another small task, completely outside my range of duties. Again, I grabbed the task and completed it to the best of my ability. A week or two later, my boss gave me another task, and then a week later, still another task.

In every case, whatever it was, whether I knew anything about it or not, I immediately went to work on it, often on my own time, and on the weekends. I would get it done and back to my boss as fast as I could.

MOVE FAST ON OPPORTUNITIES

This brings me to my second piece of advice for anyone who wants to be successful in his or her career: once you get the responsibility that you have asked for, complete it quickly and well, and get it back to your boss as fast as you can, as though it was a grenade with the pin pulled out.

Move quickly. Don't delay.

It is absolutely amazing the positive impression you will make on other people when you keep asking for more responsibility, and when you get the responsibility, you complete the task quickly. Very soon, my boss had marked me down as the "Go-to-guy."

Whenever something came up that he needed handling immediately, he called me rather than any of the other executives, some of whom had been working there for several years.

In no time, I began to move up in the organization.

BE PREPARED FOR YOUR OPPORTUNITY

One day, he threw me a task, like a football to a tight end in a close game, which I caught and ran with for a touchdown.

By acting quickly, flying a thousand miles and working day and night, I discovered a fraud and saved the company two million dollars. If I had delayed even a couple of days, the money would have been lost forever.

After that success, the dam broke. First, I was given a large assignment, and then responsibility for an entire new division, and then another new division, and then a third. By the time I had been working for that company for two years, I was running three divisions involving almost $50 million dollars worth of business activities and managing a staff of more than 50 people in three offices.

Meanwhile, my coworkers were still coming in at 9 o'clock sharp, going for lunch with each other and quitting at 5 o'clock to go for drinks at the bar. They muttered and told each other that the reason I was moving up was because I was "lucky," or the boss was playing favorites.

They never learned the importance of asking for more responsibility and moving fast.

A SECRET OF SUCCESS

The retiring president of the US Chamber of Commerce, many years ago, told a story at his going away dinner. He had become one of the most respected business people in America, and overseas. He had developed the kind of reputation for high quality work that every person in business dreams of having.

He said that when he was a young man, unsuccessful and frustrated, he came across a saying written on a brown lunch bag and posted on a high school bulletin board.

As he passed the bulletin board, something caused him to stop and he read the words on the lunch bag. They said, "Your success in life will be in direct proportion to what you do *after* you do what you are expected to do."

He told the audience that these words changed his life. Up to that time in his career, he felt that he was doing a good job because he was doing what he had been told to do, what he was expected to do.

But from that point onward, he resolved that he would do far more than what was expected of him. He resolved that he would always go the extra mile and to do more than he was paid for. From that day onward, for the rest of his career, he got up a little earlier, worked a little harder and stayed a little later.

He moved faster from task to task and from customer to customer.

And here is what always happens. The faster he moved, the more experience he got. The more experience he got, the better he got at his job. The better he got, the better results he got in the same period of time.

In no time at all, he was being paid more and promoted faster.

By moving faster and always doing more than expected, he had shifted onto the fast track in his career and began moving ahead rapidly. He was soon promoted into a new department, then hired into a new industry, and given a new area of responsibility.

In each case, he had one strategy: do more than you are paid for. Do more than others expect. Go the extra mile. Get busy. Get going. Take action. Don't waste time.

And he never looked back.

WISDOM OF A FOUNDING FATHER

Thomas Jefferson wrote, "Determine never to be idle. No person will have occasion to complain of the want of time, who never loses any. It is wonderful how much may be done, if we are always doing."

Later, he wrote, "The rising sun has never caught me in bed in my entire life."

THE TIME WILL PASS ANYWAY

Here's an important point: the time is going to pass *anyway*.

The weeks, months and years of your life are going to go by, in any case. The only question is, "What are you going to do with this time?"

Since the day is going to go past in any case, why not start a little earlier, work a little harder and stay a little later? Why not put yourself on the side of the angels? Why not develop a reputation as the "go-to-guy" (or gal) who everyone looks to when they need to get something done quickly and well?

This will do more to put your foot on the accelerator of your career than anything else you can imagine.

GET GOING AND KEEP GOING

There is a key to high income called the "Momentum Principle of Success."

This principle says that it takes considerable energy to get yourself into motion and moving. But it takes much less energy to keep yourself moving, once you get going.

This momentum principle explains success as much as any other factor. Successful people are busy people. They get up and they get going, and they keep going all day long. They work all the time they work. They are constantly in motion, like moving targets.

PLAN YOUR TIME CAREFULLY

Successful people plan their days and hours, and even their quarter-hours very carefully. In every study, there seems to be a direct relationship between tight time planning and high income.

The highest paid professionals in our society, from whom come fully 25% of self-made millionaires in America, are lawyers, doctors and other medical professionals. Every one of them manages their time in terms of *minutes* spent on each case, or with each patient.

The people who earn the very least in our society are those who think of their time in terms of the day, the week or the month. They have no problem wasting the first half of the day. They justify this by saying they will "Catch up in the afternoon."

Sometimes they waste the first couple of days of the week. They think that they will catch up later on in the week. Sometimes they waste the first one or two weeks of the month.

THE FATAL FLAW IN MONTHLY QUOTAS

I have worked with countless sales organizations over the years. Fully 80% of the salespeople in these organizations, all of whom work on monthly quotas, take it easy for the first three weeks of the month and then suddenly go into a state of frantic activity during the last week, working desperately to make enough sales to hit their quotas.

But not the top people.

The top people work on the first day of the month with the same focus and intensity that they worked on the last day of the previous month. They hit the road running, like the roadrunner, with his legs moving under him.

They put the "pedal to the metal" at seven or seven thirty in the morning. They beat the rush hour traffic by getting in before anyone else, and they beat the rush hour traffic in the evening by staying and working long after everyone else has rushed out to sit on the freeway.

GENERATE CONTINUOUS ENERGY

Mentally and physically, the faster you move, the more energy you have. The faster you move, the more positive you feel. The faster you move, the happier you are. The faster you move, the more enthusiastic and creative you become.

The faster you move the more you get done, the more you get paid and the more successful you feel.

Apply the momentum principle to your life. Once you start going, keep going. Allan Lakein, the time management specialist said, "Fast tempo is essential to success." Tom Peters said that all successful people have a "bias for action."

The key to getting more things done is for you to select your most important task and then to start it with a "Sense of urgency." This is the real key to success and high achievement.

Do Something Every Day:

1. Resolve today to pick up the pace in your life. Move faster from task to task. Walk quickly. Develop a higher tempo of activity.

2. Imagine you were going away tomorrow for a month and you had to get caught up on everything before you left. Work as hard and as fast as you do just before you leave for vacation.

3. Practice tight time planning. Imagine that you only had half the time available to get the job done and work with a sense of urgency all day long.

4. Continually ask for more responsibility, and when you get it, complete the task quickly and well. This one habit will continually open doors of opportunity for you.

From now on, resolve to get up one hour earlier and get going immediately. Work through lunchtime and coffee breaks. Stay an hour later to get caught up and ready for the next day. These additions will double your productivity and put you on the fast track in your career.

About Brian

Brian Tracy is one of the top business experts and trainers in the world. He has taught more than 5,000,000 sales people in 80 countries.

He is the President of Brian Tracy International, committed to teaching ambitious individuals how to rapidly increase their sales and personal incomes.

CHAPTER 2

THE COURAGE TO LEAD

BY ROBIN BURK, PhD

If you want to win, you must have the courage to lead. And make no mistake – leading does require courage. Fortunately, there's a process you can follow to lead with effectiveness and maximize your results.

I learned an embarrassing but invaluable lesson about leading early in my career. I'd been recruited by the founder of an early stage company to build a new business area in computing. He made it clear I would have a free hand. He would limit himself to managing existing customers until contracts ended. In return he wanted major growth and profitability.

Big challenge. Big opportunity. In essence, a re-start of the company. Many entrepreneurs have a hard time delegating and others have unrealistic expectations of instant success. So, I talked with his current employees, with recent customers of the company, and made a very discreet inquiry with someone I knew in a current client. I also asked for and got high level financial statements to review.

Eventually I signed on and the owner transferred three existing employees to my new 'division'. One left shortly afterwards, annoyed at being passed over for a promotion. That left me, plus two staff busy on existing customer projects.

The company had no external investors, so marketing and sales were my first priority before I could build a staff. I met with existing clients and dozens of potential new customers. I carefully took note of what they said – and of what they didn't say.

Then I got to work writing sales proposals. At first, our growth was dizzying. Within eighteen months we had multiple multi-year professional service contracts and our team grew to over fifty-five people, most of whom were covered by contract revenues for at least a year going forward.

The services we offered were diverse and so were the team's skills. About thirty-five team members were relatively junior people who performed technical services at customer sites. Another dozen or so were programmers who worked in our office. And four were more senior engineers whose work was crucial for positioning us as credible suppliers to sophisticated customers.

After the first year, I promoted one senior engineer to manage that group and hired two new managers: an older programmer to manage the programming group, and a recently retired Army major to manage the large group of young, onsite service providers.

We were positioned for growth and profitability going forward. I was certain of it. Most of our contracts included a provision that upped our profit based on client evaluation of our work and we were scoring very high. Staff morale was great. The company president was happy and, true to his word, stepped back from day to day operations. We met monthly to discuss progress and strategy.

And that's when I almost destroyed it all.

Initial progress secured, it was time to take a longer-term view. The tech world changes rapidly and we were addressing a wide range of technologies already. We were doing well but were in danger of aiming too broadly and with too thin a staff and customer base. How could we stay on top of opportunities, head off problems, and make sure we didn't get complacent? I was also concerned about developing the managers who reported to me. I wanted to be sure that they had real input into our direction and growth.

So, I decided the group managers and I should adopt a collaborative decision-making approach. Each month we'd review current status, identify possible new work to bid on, decide on new hires, and shape the future growth of the division. I would coordinate our process but not control it.

Do you see the cliff we were rushing blindly towards?

At first things seemed to be going smoothly. The group managers stepped out with new enthusiasm. We identified several potential new projects, bid on two, and won both. One project expanded our onsite technical support. We easily hired several new junior employees to staff it. Because the former Army major managing that group had developed a structured way to ensure quality control of the services we provided, the new junior staff fit in quickly.

Staffing the second contract proved more difficult. We needed a programmer with specific, somewhat older skills. The hiring market was tight and the technology was shifting quickly. To make things worse, there was a big difference in the pay levels that different skill sets commanded.

So, we needed to be very clear about exactly what we were seeking. Did we want a lower paid employee who could fulfill this contract position immediately but whose skills did not position us for being competitive as customers changed their technology demands? Or should we stretch and view this hire as a down payment on continued future growth at the expense of lower profits on this contract? Was it even possible for us to attract a more skilled programmer who was willing to do the less exciting work we needed right now?

The group managers had very different perspectives on this issue. The former Army major stressed the importance of clear job description and role expectations for the new hire. The leader of the small engineering group, who held a graduate degree in computer science from a leading university, stressed the implications of recent tech developments for future skill needs. And the older-but-not-so-technically-current group leader who would manage this new hire had a hard time deciding which direction to take.

We finally hired a programmer with the required skills for the immediate task. But none of us was entirely satisfied with the decision.

The damage had begun.

Slowly, the collaborative relationships between the three managers began to erode. There were no open conflicts, but a deepening weariness set in. The bright future we were creating seemed farther and farther away, and less and less certain. Obstacles now loomed in high relief. It was like air seeping slowly out of a balloon. And a subtle demoralization spread across the whole staff.

On paper we were doing fine. Our numbers looked great. But I had a growing unease about the whole situation.

That's when the leader of the engineering group knocked on my open door and asked to speak with me privately. Liu grew up in an Asian culture. He was a quiet, powerful asset to our team. But I had never seen him do what he did when he entered my office that day.

He bowed deeply to me.

My heart sank. This is it, I thought – Liu's resigning. Oh no!

To my relief, Liu wasn't resigning. Instead he closed the door behind him and sat down. Then he quietly but firmly told me he was there to respectfully remind me to do my job. To lead the division so that he, his engineers, and the other groups could do their own jobs more effectively.

It is the single most important, helpful thing anyone ever said to me in my career, before or since. It led to my ongoing success. And it can lead to yours as well.

That afternoon I let the group managers know that I would be resuming responsibility for business planning, final hire approval, and bid decisions. I would seek their inputs and had every confidence that they would manage their groups effectively in executing the plan. But I would once again lead the division.

I would do my job.

TO LEAD REQUIRES COURAGE

Leading is hard. Many entrepreneurs never get the hang of it. They refuse to delegate. Or they refuse to make hard decisions. They are the ones who fail... whose companies limp along but never grow rapidly, return high profits, or attract buyers when the founder wants to cash out.

To lead you must take informed risks, make clear decisions, select the right people, and motivate them to help you put those decisions into effect. You must be willing to delegate implementation while retaining responsibility for the overall outcome of your decisions. You must establish an organization that is both flexible and has sufficient structure to allow employees to scope their daily and weekly tasks effectively.

And that requires transitioning from a founder mindset to the habits and skills a leader requires. It means building a team, establishing operating procedures, and holding yourself to the discipline of working through them.

Becoming a leader is hard. But there is a five step process you can follow again and again, to succeed as a leader and win in the market.

Step One: Set and regularly review goals.

If you don't know where you want to get to, chances are you won't arrive there.

Effective leaders develop the habit of setting clear, measurable, and meaningful goals. Goals translate your overall vision into specific outcomes you intend to achieve by a given date. Meaningful goals are key to bringing your vision into being.

Entrepreneurial companies usually set quantitative financial goals. For instance, you might target quarterly revenues of $XX at a profit margin of YY% in the third quarter, or to increase annual sales by ZZ% by the end of the year.

Whatever goals you set, be realistic even as you are ambitious. To be an effective leader you will need to communicate those goals in convincing ways to your employees in order to succeed.

Step Two: Evaluate your starting place.

Pick your key goal. Now take an honest look at your company's current position with regard to it. How close are you to achieving that goal today? What are your company's current strengths? What are its weaknesses?

What new resources does the company need in order to succeed at this goal? Resources include cash flow or financing, personnel, equipment and other internal elements. But they also can include channel partners, suppliers, new customers, and importantly, information. How well do you really know the demand and concerns of your current customers? Of potential new customers?

Make a plan to acquire tangible resources you will need to succeed at this goal. And then move on to Step Three to gather the information you need.

Step Three: Listen.

Before you make a decision about how to proceed toward your goal, listen carefully to the various stake holders that might be affected. What do your employees think are the obstacles and opportunities the decision must address? What do your current customers think about your company, your offerings, and especially about their unmet needs and your competition?

If you have outside investors or are networked with potential investors, listen to their perspective on the markets, competition, and operational factors relevant to your decision, as well. Getting their perspective – whether you agree with them or not – can help clarify the decision you need to make.

Step Four: Decide on an action plan.

You've set an important goal, evaluated your starting place, and acquired needed resources including information. Now you must have the courage to make an unambiguous decision about the plan the company will execute in order to achieve it. Weigh the risks and upsides, and then decide.

Step Five: Act.

Once you've decided, it's time to put your plan to work. Clearly communicate your goal to the staff and the actions each employee must take. Give them unambiguous objectives and then allow them to do their own jobs.

Make sure the plan includes regular evaluations of progress and obstacles. Employees might uncover important new information. New competition might enter your market. Or you might need to adjust to unexpected levels of success.

Plans can and should change in response. At any given time, however, everyone in your company should know what you are working towards, why it's important, and what steps they should be taking now.

THE PAYOFF FOR COURAGE

It takes courage to commit to clear decisions and take risks, to delegate, even (especially, sometimes) to set meaningful goals. But the payoff is worth it.

Leaders sometimes make decisions that fail. Just be sure that you know what your goal and decision are at any given moment and be ready to shift – but not flail – when need be.

It's the path to winning in the market and in life.

So set goals, evaluate your situation regularly, listen carefully, decide, and act with clarity. Adjust when circumstances change. Lead effectively and your company – and the market – will follow.

About Robin

From her early days writing code in Silicon Valley through her time as an entrepreneur, executive, and consultant, Dr. Robin Burk has been on the cutting edge of change. She's had bottom line P&L responsibility, managed diverse workforces, started two companies, taught university level students, and consulted to business owners and executives.

Today her mission is to help people and businesses thrive in the face of rapid, technology-driven change and the uncertainty it brings.

Robin is an expert in how the complex systems we rely on work – what makes the internet, banking system, international markets, and supply chains robust or vulnerable. This gives her unique insight into challenges and opportunities business face today.

She holds an MBA in finance and operations and a PhD in information science (machine learning, artificial intelligence and data analysis). Her undergraduate degree in liberal arts has been a valuable career asset as well.

Robin has worked in Silicon Valley, southern California, the Research Triangle Park, northern Virginia and New York as well as the Midwest, and done business in Europe, the Middle East and Asia. After the attacks of 9/11/2001 she taught at West Point for 7 years before growing a fledgling effort into a highly innovative, effective research program in complex systems at the Defense Threat Reduction Agency. She then turned the program over to a young manager and built a new capability in complex systems and decision analysis at another major organization before launching her current initiative.

Robin is the author of best-selling books for technical professionals and of the recent book *Check Your Connections: How to Thrive in an Uncertain World* (Voynich Press). She has been quoted in places like *Wired, A Girl's Guide to Project Management* and the *Small Business Experts Forum*, appeared multiple times on national television, and been featured on dozens of radio shows across the US and Canada. In April of 2018 Robin gave her first TEDx talk.

In her free time she loves to garden, to take long walks with her dogs, and to travel with her husband Roger.

She can be reached through inquiries at:

- http://checkyourconnections.com

For consulting in the use of advanced analytics and big data for business advantage, at:

- http://analyticdecisions2.com

CHAPTER 3

DOMESTICATING FEAR TO OBTAIN THE KEY TO SUCCESS

BY PETER WOLFING

When I was a recruit in USMC boot camp, we were taught that 90% of overcoming any obstacle is preparation. Only 10% is the actual plan. Staff Sergeant Thornton (I'll never forget his name) taught us that pliability and flexibility in battle situations are the keys to overcoming obstacles. Being able to calmly look at a specific situation and decide what you can and can't control and then looking at various perspectives to uncover possible solutions is a strategy to win any battle and become successful.

Unfortunately, this way of thinking is not in our nature as human beings. Fear can grab hold and freeze even the strongest person in their tracks. It's a reflex action to protect us from harm. But, this initial wave of fear is only momentary. What comes after that is what is counter-productive to the situation.

That's where we were taught to domesticate fear. Let me describe what I mean. What does domesticate rejection (fear) mean? Most of us have had a dog. When you first get a dog, it can be wild and untamed often reacting with its internal instinct to give into situations without thinking. It's a base instinct in an animal's nature and a mechanism for survival. Out in the wild, in situations of life or death, instinct can save its life.

Domesticating the dog means you train them to react the way you want them to react in given situations. Domesticated animals react more predictably. This "fear instinct" is also in us. Our brain reacts instantly through our subconscious which triggers motor-responses to our physical body – fight-or-flight kicks in. When we are afraid, we usually have a burst of high emotion, and many of our physical functions are put on hold. Things like rational thought and even blood to our extremities are directed inward toward vital organs. Have you ever heard the saying, "My blood ran cold."? That's what is happening.

Your goal (as it was for me in boot camp) is to domesticate the fear. In the US Marines, this was so that if we ever went into a battlefield, we would run towards the danger and not away from it, in order to continue and hopefully win the fight. The domestication of fear is no different in our personal and business life.

How do we react to challenging bosses or co-workers? How do we react to rejection from prospects, clients or job interviews? Can we turn the situation into a positive by seeing the situation in a different perspective? How do we turn rejection and fear into things to learn from?

When you practice domesticating your fear around such rejections, you are training yourself to react in an orderly, non-instinctive way. Thus, the way you react to fear is trained and not that knee-jerk instinctive reaction. When we domesticate rejection, we make it completely powerless over us, and we start to seek it out. We see it as the obstacle to go through something which makes us stronger and reach our goals faster.

The next step is to seek out the origin of our fears. To domesticate them, we need to understand where they are coming from. The conscious mind can accept or reject any idea, but the information stored in your subconscious mind will, to an enormous degree, control what your conscious mind will accept or reject, as well your perception of it. In short - our perception is filtered through our beliefs.

The vital bit that many people don't realize is that it's their old conditioning that is causing them to reject the idea! Our reasoning ability and logic is a conditioned response. What we want to do is decondition (domesticate) our thinking. Think about that for a moment - our ability to reason, to be objective, is also conditioned. We select the logic to match the conditioning.

When we're in our comfort zone, we experience comfortable thoughts, influenced by our comfortable conditioning, which leads to comfortable actions which lead to the same results. That conditioning limits our thoughts and keeps us from succeeding or growing. Just outside the comfort zone is the terror barrier, this is the point where we are subject to a flow of negative, unhealthy emotions. It's that feeling of dread, that certainty that we are doomed which wells up when we think of doing something that we are scared of doing - even if we want to do it. All of this is an automatic response by our body. Even if we think it's safe intellectually when our body experiences this feeling it will convince us the last thing in the world we want to do is continue.

Whenever anyone steps outside their comfort zone there are four stages that they go through.

1. Comfort (I'm happy where I am)
2. Reason (Actually, I want more than this)
3. Terror (Oh my Goodness, I can't do it; I'm not good enough)
4. Freedom (Oh, actually I can do it … wow!)

Most people don't reach the freedom stage. To get past the terror stage (or terror barrier), we must first change our beliefs so we can clearly and objectively see the situation. Back in boot camp, Staff Sergeant Thornton knew this, and through teaching, understanding, and repetition, we were able to overcome our natural instincts.

The emotion or fear response stems from the activating event, i.e., whatever it is that we are thinking of doing. The activating event doesn't have to be an act; it can also be a feeling or a thought - real or imagined. The key thing to understanding the response is that the body doesn't respond directly to the activating event, it responds to our belief about the activating event! Our conditioning is made up of a mass of beliefs. Beginning to form an understanding of the process and see what's happening will create the power to move forward despite the feeling.

So, there you are, you're in your comfort zone, taking life easy and this unexpressed possibility (desire) begins to bubble up inside of you. You become aware of what Emerson called "that quiet voice within" and you think to yourself, "You know, I don't want to live like this anymore. I want more than this. I don't care what the rest of you are doing!" Then, you begin to entertain that new desire. You're now entering the 'reason' stage. As you begin to focus on this new desire, your new idea moves into the subconscious mind, and it's then that you move to stage 3, terror.

As the new idea ferments, it begins to change the vibration of your body and creates a 'foreign vibration.' At first, your comfortable conditioning begins to whisper to you, "What are you doing? Are you serious? What makes you think you can do this? Who do you think you are?" Your conditioning is devious; it's insidious. It will do anything to talk you out of the new desire because if you do this, everything changes, and it doesn't like change.

So next, your conditioning turns to reason. You begin to have arguments with yourself. Things like, "Look, you've given it your best shot, there's no disgrace in turning back now. Let's go back now to how it was, just you and me". Then, as you seriously consider taking action on your new desire, the old comfortable conditioning begins to scream at you. Fear knows exactly what buttons to push and where your Achilles heels are. More thoughts flood through you, things like, "Don't you remember what happened last time you tried something like this? How ridiculous you looked? I'd like to support you in this, I really would but I'll be honest with you, I don't think you'll ever recover if you screw this up like you normally do."

This cycle happens in a heartbeat, as you give serious consideration to taking action. Within milliseconds you start to worry. Doubt fills your conscious mind. That worry is experienced in the mind as fear, and it's expressed in the body as anxiety. Your blood runs cold. Terror fills every cell of your body, and before you know what's happened, you bounce right off the terror barrier and back into your comfort zone.

When you're suddenly faced with a challenge that is new to you, it's amazing how just a simple idea can turn from butterflies, into terror, into "I think I need to go to the bathroom!"

Then, you're back here safely in our comfort zone, recovering, saying, "My goodness, that was close." We don't like to admit to ourselves that we got scared and ran away. We immediately begin to rationalize, to justify our actions. "Well, I didn't want it. I don't think the money is as good as I thought it was going to be. They're not nice people in that industry. To be honest, it isn't what I really want to do; I'll find something better. I'm just glad I've got the courage to stand up and say this is not what I want. I think a lot of people wouldn't have been able to do that." We convince ourselves that our act of cowardice was actually one of bravery! We convince ourselves that we are happy where we are.

So how do we break through the terror barrier to freedom? It takes one of two things:

1. Your goal is something that you want so badly; it's worth failing for.

2. It takes just one, tiny additional ingredient, one tiny little thing that will give you the courage to step through that terror barrier when you bump up against it and that one missing thing is understanding.

UNDERSTANDING LEADS TO THE DOMESTICATION OF FEAR

Once you recognize that the fear is not real, you're off to the races. Fear is just conscious awareness of the vibration that your body and your life are heading in a whole new direction. The old conditioning never really goes away, but as you impress a new idea, it gradually starts to take on more and more energy, as Emerson said, "The only thing that can grow is the thing we give energy to. If we feed our fear, give it energy, it will grow. If we feed our idea, it will grow. If we feed our confidence, then it will grow. We don't need to give fear its consciousness."

How do you get rid of the dark in a room? You change the perception by turning on the light, right? You don't focus on the dark and try to get rid of it. You think of light and introduce light. The light displaces the dark. So too can confidence displace crippling fear. Of course, it's still scary to some degree on an emotional level, but it's manageable. If we don't feed fear, then confidence will win.

Let's try the same situation about that piece of understanding.

So here we are again, back in comfort. The desire inside wells up and once again we begin to give serious consideration to acting on our new idea. As the new idea is impressed upon the subconscious mind, it sets up a foreign vibration in our body. Terror fills our body, but this time we have an understanding. This time, we see the fear for what it is, just conscious awareness of the vibration our body is in, and we refuse to give it its consciousness.

Instead, we feed our confidence by focussing on the benefits of our goal. We still feel afraid but understanding gives us courage and this time we act in spite of our fear. We're able to step forward into growth and smash through the terror barrier into freedom!

Even though you've been through the terror barrier once, the fear doesn't go away. We need to continue to work through the terror barrier many more times before we begin to feel comfortable with the new way of doing things. Then, the new way becomes as comfortable as the old way once was. This is now your new comfort zone.

The domestication of fear starts from an understanding and the courage to challenge our limiting beliefs. This practice is the way in which you can achieve any goal that is set before you. When you overcome your programming, it leads to a calmness of spirit. You can now objectively see what is really there with a new perspective. With this in mind, you can change your whole life for the better.

About Peter

Peter Wolfing is not your average entrepreneur. He traces his entrepreneurial desire back to a very young age while in grade school. He's learned practical knowledge through real-world experiences. While a Sergeant in the USMC, he learned the crucial skills of leadership, delegation and problem-solving.

Peter will also be featured on Times Square TV Live to be aired on ABC, NBC, CBS, and FOX affiliates. He has close to three decades of experience creating original content in the 100-billion-dollar e-learning space.

Over the past two decades, Peter has developed many online platforms that have attracted a membership base of over 2 million people around the globe. He's mentored countless people, many of which have gone on to develop 6- and 7-figure incomes.

Peter's been called the "Uber" of his industry because he's an out-of-the-box thinker and has revolutionized the online home-based business model. Much like Uber shook the foundation of the automobile travel industry by deconstructing it and completely simplifying the model, Peter has shaken the foundation of the network marketing industry by disassembling the cumbersome infrastructure and completely streamlining the system. He has virtually re-invented the industry. The result? A more efficient, more effective, less complicated, online business model. Limited risk, high upside potential, and incredibly fast growth.

His most recent project is providing the driving force for WizKids.org, a 501(c)(3) not-for-profit charitable organization which coaches and mentors young entrepreneurs.

Peter is an expert trainer, mentor, and author of multiple books. One is co-authored with Sir Richard Branson – titled *Performance 360* – and is destined to be a bestseller.

He has just completed a new book called, *The Warrior Within Domesticating Fear* which has been endorsed by Kevin Harrington, a founding member of the hit TV show, *Shark Tank*, which can be found at: www.domesticatingfear.com.

Peter lives in Manhattan, NYC and is an in-demand speaker and trainer on such topics as leadership, communication, sales, digital products, affiliate and network marketing and he is a certified John Maxwell Team Executive Director.

Are you stuck and can't seem to break through? Peter can help you.

You can find him on Facebook, Instagram, YouTube: /peterwolfing or go to his website:

- www.peterwolfing.com

CHAPTER 4

PERSISTENCE THROUGH RELATIONSHIPS

BY ADRIAN N. HAVELOCK

The first time I was introduced to the self-development industry, I was a 19-year-old salesman at a local BMW dealership, then called Bavarian Motors Limited. The company had taken a chance in hiring me for a job that they advertised for individuals over the age of 25. They saw in me a drive and passion for the brand which I fell in love with as a kid. At one of the weekly meetings, our chairman at the time played us a VHS tape - Les Brown's Its Possible video. That video changed the course of my overall attitude, the vision I had for myself, the relationships I had with people, and ultimately, gave me the will to win.

I grew up in the nineties, in what may be considered the average household. Both parents and siblings had the average level of education in an average community on the tropical island of Trinidad. At the time, self-development teachings were not as popular as they are now. As a result of seeing that video, I was driven to push my life into a direction I had never previously envisioned.

Our parents, educators and Sunday school teachers taught us their version of what it means to "be successful". This entailed doing the right things, helping others, getting a good job, buying a home, having a family, and then starting over the cycle. No one inspired me to be different, pursue my passions and live a full life while growing up. I only knew what I knew, and I didn't know what I didn't know, because I was limited by the dated knowledge and experience of my parents and teachers. That type of limitation still exists, maintaining the boundaries on today's generation.

I remember when I was about 13 years old, my mother was having a conversation with me and one of her colleagues from the church. The topic of conversation was my career path post-secondary education. The best option for me, as they saw it, was that I continue being active in the Presbyterian church so that I could apply for work as a teacher through the assistance of the church at a Presbyterian school. It was a respected profession, and their opinion was that many people who started their careers as teachers ended spending their professional life in that one place, because the benefits were good, hours were shorter than a regular job, and was steady and safe.

Back then, I was furious because I did not want to be a teacher. Now, I am not discounting the profession nor am I against it, but it was not who I wanted to be. My mother and her colleague's limited knowledge and experience siloed their understanding of what it meant to be successful. Today I am a teacher, but not in the conventional sense. My work inspires others to do their best through speaking, training and development of skills for becoming successful in life.

Very early in my professional journey, I learnt the art of working towards small wins in an effort to achieve the big win in life. In 2007, I came across the teachings of Dr. Norman Vincent Peale, and was inspired to read his internationally-acclaimed book, *The Power of Positive Thinking.* This book hit me as hard as a boomerang would on its return after throwing it. This book had such an impact on my life that I started performing better in my sales at BMW, and immediately shot up to be in the top three performers of the company until I resigned. The teachings I believe, gave me the inspiration, drive, will, motivation, confidence and courage to go after the things that I wanted, the relationships I wanted to build, the independent life I wanted to live and the belief that I could be the person I wanted to become.

Here are some of the lines in the book that stood out to me:
- *I found in them an answer to my own problems and believe me, I am the most difficult person with whom I have ever worked.*
- *Attitudes are more important than fact.*
- *I can do all things through Christ which strengthens me.* (Philippians 4:13)
- *If God be for us, who can be against us.* (Romans 8:31)
- *I didn't go to bed with an ear full of trouble, I went to sleep with a mind full of peace.*
- *We manufacture our own unhappiness.*
- *People are defeated in life not because of lack of ability, but for lack of wholeheartedness. They do not wholeheartedly expect to succeed.*
- *Throw your heart over the bar and your body will follow.*

Through this book, I have since learnt the application of the scientific processes of how to acknowledge that whatever I pray for in conversation with God, to believe I have already received it and hold onto that feeling. The vibrations I sent out send a message to the universe through the power of God utilising the vibrations in everything that surrounds us, to live in harmony with all that goes on around us. There is good and bad, and one must have faith that all will work out in the end. And it always does.

This book taught me how to truly develop a close relationship with God and I strongly recommend it's teachings no matter your religion, or even if you do not believe in religion. The experiences in the book, it's tips and tutorials are all practical and are explained using science, psychology and facts. I was able to understand that in this life, worry is the most subtle and destructive of all human diseases. I learnt that fear is the most disintegrating enemy of human personality, and as Dr. Smiley Blanton says, anxiety is the great modern plague but faith can cure it. To this day, this is my #1 book for inspiration and I read it every year to recharge my confidence batteries.

When I left BMW as a salesman, my drive and motivation I had built up over the years gave me the confidence to start something new. Something I always wanted to do – start my own business. Over the years, I had taken short business courses because they seemed practical to me as teachings that were applicable to life. Not knowing what kind of business to start and without a job, I thought to myself, *"What is the one thing I am good at that I can make money with?"* Immediately I knew, I could sell.

Through extensive research and focus, I was able to build out a presentation about my sales approach using my experiences and learnings. It was at that point I decided that I needed my own space to host workshops. It was a bad investment. After spending valuable resources on renovating the space and outfitting it with equipment, I recognized after two months that I had taken on unnecessary debt that would not yield any returns. I quickly adopted a leaner approach to business, and transitioned to a home office. It was my most expensive failure to date. It was a hard lesson for me to learn that at that time, nobody knew who I was, nor would anyone be willing to pay for my workshops or for sales advice.

Times have changed and today my name is recognised as the go-to corporate sales trainer in Trinidad. But take a look at what I had to learn for it to happen. Initial plans to set up workshop space was not successful, but it didn't mean I needed to change my plan and go back to being an employee. All it meant was that I needed to change my course of action. Barbara Bush said *"When you come to a roadblock, take a detour."* That's what I did. Instead of having people come to 'my office' for training, I went to their companies to train their staff.

The will to win isn't about trying new things every time you get a burst of inspiration and stopping when things don't work, or don't seem to work immediately. The will to win is about having faith in yourself, your abilities and your goals, even if that faith is as small as a mustard seed. It is about being persistent and consistent.

I remember visiting the offices of the largest manufacturer of labels, print and digital media for the Caribbean region. It is one of the most innovative and forward-moving organisations I have worked with called the Label House Group of companies. The directors took a chance with me in my earlier days as a sales trainer to come in and work with their staff. Perhaps it was my will to win that got me through the door? In the first email I ever received from Mr Richard Lewis, he said:

"Adrian I do not normally reply to emails of this kind but it would be interesting to see if you really have the ability to help with the sales of a company that we have as a subsidiary. Call me at 645- - - - - next week Thursday around mid-morning to set up a time that you can come in to have a chat at our office. Richard Lewis."

Both Richard and his brother David Lewis now believe in my work, as they have experienced real results. I have proven myself as a dedicated individual of service. Today, I continue to work with Richard and David's company in a consulting capacity in varying areas for Branding, Marketing and even on behalf of their group presenting to their clients who are some of the world's best known brands in the food and beverage industries. That experience gave me insight into new industries, and I was able to use that knowledge to enhance the way in which I deliver my services. A mutually-beneficial relationship was forged from inception and I have learnt from that experience how to position myself as an asset to any potential client.

Resulting from these relationships and experiences, I was also able to write my first book *You Can Do This - How to Succeed in Sales and in Life*. More importantly, I built the confidence in myself to seek out the stories of some of the world's best-selling authors according to the New York Times, Sunday Times and Amazon, such as Jim Cathcart, Andy Harrington, Tony J. Selimi, Robert Rolih. Always surround yourself with winners. Find a way to get into those winners' circles and network not for business, but for true meaningful relationships. Give value, and in return, life will continue to present you with reasons to continue striving for success.

THE B.A.P. FORMULA

I want to now share with you a formula to help you devise your own will to win. This three part system is easy to remember and follow. I call it the B.A.P. formula.

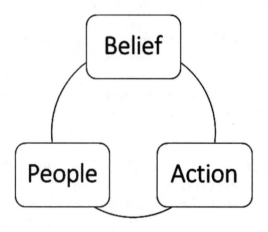

Believe in yourself
Start surrounding yourself with motivational material such as books, videos, podcasts, webinars, courses, events. Anything that you know will have a positive impact in your life. Take the teachings and put them to use. Too many times people go for what is entertaining and not substantial in growing or expanding their minds and hearts.

Action

Take action towards your goals. Yes, you see the big picture. Yes, it looks intimidating. So break it down into smaller goals and work your way up by achieving those smaller goals no matter the time it would take to achieve them. Action teaches you how to deal with failure by giving you that experience of failure. The will to win comes from trying again. Do you think I'd be here today writing this content with these other great authors in this book if I had stopped at the point when I closed my workshop space? Take action, make mistakes and learn how to do it better the next time you try.

People

Jim Rohn once said, *"You are the average of the five people you spend the most time with."* He wasn't lying. My associations with my past BMW clients and my newfound friends and clients help me move up as they are all people who I consider more successful than I am. They are people who I can learn from. They are people who are encouraging whenever you share an idea. Someone successful can always tell you how you can do it. Unsuccessful people or people who have never done it before tell you all the ways it will not work. My relationships, both locally and on an international level, have helped me in many ways to become a better person and to treat others well, not to judge, be open-minded, patient and aware of my thoughts – negative or positive.

Follow the B.A.P formula and begin today your journey to success! I know you have it in you, I know your goals are right around the corner past the next failure. Keep the faith and know that if God be for you, who can possibly be against you?

YOU HAVE THE WILL TO WIN!

About Adrian

Adrian N. Havelock helps corporate giants and their staff communicate with their customers in a non-salesy way. His method has made him one of the most sought-after sales trainers in the Caribbean.

He started his career as an assistant to a sales representative within the Insurance industry, then made his own breakthrough in sales at the young age of 19 at the local franchise of BMW in Trinidad. He was the youngest car salesman in the country at that time, and it was at BMW that he mastered the art of sales and the sales process. His passion for excellence and dedication to serve his customers resulted in him earning a spot in the top three sales performers by the age of 22.

Driven by passion to educate customers on the benefits and values of products pivoted Adrian's career to Training and Development. He lives by the philosophy: *Selling – It's Simple Communication.* He started off unofficially coaching staff and colleagues on the products being sold, which established the foundation for his move into corporate sales training, branding and marketing consultancy.

Adrian believes that transforming one company at a time can make a difference in building valuable people. His teachings have helped hundreds of people increase relationships and build strong businesses. His accolades include Business Consultant for Sales Training, Branding and Marketing, and Regional Instructor for BMW in Product and Technology with KAPTA (Bogota, Colombia). Adrian is also the Creative Executive Producer for a local television series dedicated to overall wellness, health and fitness in Trinidad.

In the past five years, Adrian has amassed extensive experience in industries such as Finance, Energy/ Oil and Gas, Manufacturing, Labels, Packaging and Branding, Out of Home Advertising media, Electronics, Gambling, Fast Food Restaurants, Business Publications, Automotive and Retail. He is a National Speaker who has shared insights on various topics including motivation, sales, health and wellness.

You can connect with Adrian at:

- www.adrianhavelock.com
- www.adriannhavelock.com
- www.linkedin.com/in/adrian-n-havelock-80361917
- https://www.facebook.com/AdrianNHavelock/
- https://twitter.com/Adrianhavelock
- https://www.instagram.com/adrian.n.havelock/

CHAPTER 5

CHOOSE TO WIN!

BY BELINDA GOODRICH

Two roads diverged in a wood, and I – I took the one less traveled by, and that has made all the difference.
~ Robert Frost, *The Road Not Taken*

"You will never go to college… you probably won't even graduate from high school."

These words were said to me my sophomore year in high school, cutting through my very heart and soul. From the time I was a little girl, my dream was to go to college and to be a doctor. But even more than taking away my dream, those words hurt because of who it was that said them: my favorite guidance counselor at my high school.

Rewind a few weeks and his words to me were very different. We talked about my SAT scores (that were fantastic!) and the list of colleges that I was eyeing. But in less than 30 days our dialog changed. Why? Because I was pregnant at 16 years old. The shame, fear, and disappointment I felt was only magnified by the reactions of the adults around me. I had let everyone down. My guidance counselor's voice echoed in my head and in my heart.

But there was another voice. The voice of my step-father. A man not known to be kind or patient. A man fighting his own demons. And yet just when I needed it, his words and actions literally changed my life and set me on the path to entrepreneurial success.

SAVED BY ICE CREAM

We lived in a small town in Maine where my mother and step-father operated a child-care center. I was raised working there and was taught to work hard. A few days after that heart-breaking talk with my guidance counselor, my step-father offered a lifeline to me: he asked me to run another business in our town for the summer.

Standish is a quintessential New England town, boasting, at the time, one stop light, a handful of variety stores, and access to arguably one of the most beautiful lakes in New England. Standish also had an ice cream stand on the main road. My step-father, with a wisdom that I did not come to appreciate until many years later, decided that running the ice cream stand for the summer would be good for me.

Despite not having any extra money, my step-father signed the lease and gave the deposit. The only stipulation was that I handle all aspects of managing the business: designing the menu, ordering the food and equipment, managing staff, and handling the finances. I knew I could not let him down.

It was a cold and rainy summer that year, but I was able to deliver a great product, hire dedicated staff (that were, ironically, my high school peers), and manage the finances to ensure that all bills and wages were paid. Those eight weeks gave me back some pride, some integrity, and they certainly fueled my desire to succeed. I started my junior year very pregnant and very focused. I was made stronger and prouder through that summer.

LESSONS FOR SUCCESS

Fast-forward almost thirty years: I have a thriving and rapidly-growing business, I have published multiple books, I have earned advanced degrees, and I enjoy my beautiful family that includes three grown daughters and six grandchildren.

I had the opportunity to reflect on what exactly made the difference in my career, and it all goes back to that ice cream stand in that small town. I sat down with my "dad" and asked him what he was thinking, entrusting a messed-up 16-year-old with a relatively risky business venture. His immediate response was, "Well, you needed to support that baby, didn't you?" But after a minute he went deeper. He explained that he *knew* what I was capable of and he wanted *me* to know that for myself.

Pregnant or not, to him, I was still the same smart, capable, and driven young lady that I was before I got pregnant. He said it was simple: "I exploited your strengths to remove you from your *perceived* weaknesses. I needed to give you a win in your column. I knew you were going to make it a success and if it was a failure, you were going to learn some business lessons. Lessons that were much more important in life than what you were hearing at your high school."

As a matter of fact, that summer left with me seven lessons that I have consistently applied to grow my businesses since then, and to help other entrepreneurs grow their businesses:

<u>Lesson One:</u> Don't be afraid to take chances.

"Change or remain the same."

If you are not happy, satisfied, and profitable in your current role, position, or business condition, then it is time that you take that leap of faith, that big step, toward your new future. Best case scenario, you are wildly successful. Worst case scenario, you fail, and you learn some great lessons.

When my training and consulting firm settled into a consistent profitable operation, I decided to take a chance and open a restaurant in my home town as a side business. For the record, restaurants are not side businesses! The venture was a dismal failure and I certainly felt the pain financially. But, after the dust settled and the debts were paid, I can honestly say it was an incredible learning experience that only made me a stronger business woman.

What have you learned from your failures?

<u>Lesson Two:</u> Make the risks big enough to apply pressure.

"Go big or go home."

Without consequences, we tend not to take action. You want to put enough at risk that you feel the pressure to perform. I recognized that there were a lot of people depending on me to do well that summer: my yet-to-be born daughter and my parents. I was very aware that my parents did not have disposable income to support a bad business venture. I resolved to do everything to ensure that the business was a success.

Without some type of deadline or other pressing constraint, we flounder. Do you know which day of the week is most productive for project teams in business environments? According to research, it is Thursday. Why? Because status reports are typically due on Friday. This is known as "student syndrome." In other words, people procrastinate. Parkinson's Law states that "work expands so as to fill the time available for its completion." This also applies to the concept of consequences. If you don't fear the consequence, you won't do the work.

What is motivating you to get the work done?

Lesson Three: Eat your product.

"Nom, nom, nom!"

It does not sound like a bad problem to have, right? Open an ice cream stand and eat the ice cream! As a pregnant teenager, I did not have any problem indulging in a creamy delicious treat daily. However, this lesson is not about the simple enjoyment of ice cream. It's about finding your *product* delicious!

To be successful in business, you must absolutely love your product. So much so, in fact, that it is evident to everyone you encounter. Your love and passion for your product should be contagious to others. My husband once said to me, "I love the days you are in the training room!" "Why is that?" I asked. He replied, "because on those days you absolutely shine. It is evident that you love what you do."

Does your job make you shine?

Lesson Four: Have faith in yourself and know others have faith in you.

"Walk by faith."

It all came down to faith, didn't it? The faith that my step-father had in me. The faith that I developed in myself. And the faith that my guidance counselor did *not* have in me. High school is hard enough for a teenager. The torment, sideways glances, and nasty rumors brought me to tears constantly. But for each time I was broken down with an unkindness, I became stronger.

My strength and resolve grew with each victory. And my step-father's faith in me allowed me to have opportunities for victories and to be successful. As I started to ratchet up some wins, my faith in myself increased. Don't get me wrong. I still struggle with imposter syndrome periodically. But I use that negative voice inside me to conjure up my strength and recognize that even if my faith in myself is wavering, I can take those first few shaky steps because my family has faith in me.

Do you have faith in yourself?

Lesson Five: Location, location, location.

"On the road again!"

Every summer, the people of Quebec migrate down to the coast of Maine for summer holidays. There is one road that connects Quebec to the southern Maine coast: Route 25. Despite being a small town, Standish witnesses a swell of traffic as the Canadiens make their way to their vacation destination. And that traffic went right past the ice cream stand. I was in the perfect location to attract traffic. Adding a sign that 'We Speak French / Parlez-vous Francais' placed out front – further attracted our Canadian customers.

In today's market, location is not just the physical location. It is being visible to your customers and clients where they can see you on *their* route, such as via their social media channels. Being accessible to your clients also means being able to speak their language, not expecting them to speak yours. Make it easy for your customer-base to do business with you.

Do your customers see you and do you speak their language?

Lesson Six: It is when you are at your worst, that you have the best opportunity to shine.

"There's gotta be a little rain sometime!"

The day I received the keys to the ice cream stand I was broken but optimistic. I had hit rock-bottom as a 16-year old pregnant girl from a small town in Maine. Somehow, I recognized that there was only one way to go: up. And so up I went.

It is often said that the best customer service comes after the worst customer experiences. Think of a customer service experience you had where your loyalty increased to a company by the way they handled a bad situation. Recovery is so much more powerful than the status quo. It is time that we change the perspective of failure as a negative and begin viewing it as an opportunity. Working out at the gym tears our muscles so that they get stronger. That is exactly how we should consider our failures in business and in life. We are stitched back together even stronger.

Do you view your low points as an opportunity to have the greatest growth?

<u>Lesson Seven:</u> Remember, it is only a season.

"To everything there is a season."

In Maine, our lives are dictated by our seasons. They are all powerful and purposeful. Fall fills the air with the smell of woodstoves and the bright colors of the autumn leaves. Winter comes in with a deep freeze, short days, and frost heaves. Spring brings beautiful renewal and lots of mud. And alas! Summer - perhaps the most coveted season in New England. But Maine is fickle, and she is never predictable when it comes to summer. Hot, sunny days are the impetus for buying ice cream. The summer I ran the ice cream stand was notoriously rainy and cold. Despite the challenges of the season, I was still able to be successful although not as profitable had the rain stayed away.

Those nine months of pregnancy at the high school seemed excruciatingly long, and it was rare that I could glimpse what life would be like after school. But it did end. It was simply a cold and rainy season. And now when I look back, I realize just how short of a season it was. And my business failure and recovery? Again, a season. A season to learn a powerful lesson that would enable me to be successful in my future endeavors.

Do you embrace your seasons?

CONCLUSION

Our lives are a beautiful tapestry of experiences: victories, failures, struggles, and successes. When we begin to consider all those experiences as necessary for growth, our perspective changes. What is your ice cream stand?

About Belinda

Belinda Goodrich is globally recognized as a project management expert. She is the founder and CEO of The Goodrich Institute and PM Learning Solutions. Under The Goodrich Institute, Belinda serves as a consultant and facilitator to companies across multiple industries. Her focus is on improving project management processes and practices in order to drive business growth. PM Learning Solutions provides world-class project management and exam preparation training programs and materials.

Belinda's entrepreneurial roots run deep. She was raised working at a family-run business. She managed her first business at 16, and at 20 opened her own business in direct competition with her parents. After graduating from college, she brought her drive for business growth and success to Corporate America in positions of increasing responsibility. With over 20 years of corporate project management and executive leadership experience, Belinda "retired" to serve the business community through consultation and facilitation in 2008.

The first woman in the world to achieve five of the Project Management Institute (PMI) credentials, Belinda now holds the following credentials: PMP®, CAPM®, PMI-SP®, PMI-ACP®, PMI-RMP®, PgMP®. With a focus on organizational psychology, Belinda is fascinated with the mind, emotions, and behaviors of organizations and team members, and she leverages that fascination to develop practical applications for business, process, and project management techniques.

An accomplished speaker, Belinda brings her practical experience, her knack for storytelling, and her Maine humor (and accent!) to audiences across all industries. *The Goodrich Model of Project Management Excellence* (P5) has been implemented by a number of firms, resulting in significant cost savings and quality improvements. P5 is an in-depth evaluation of an organization's People, Products, Processes, Purpose, and Passion.

As the author of courseware on project management and PMI exam topics, Belinda is an in-demand facilitator. Belinda has helped thousands of project managers achieve their project management credentials. Her passion is creating the connection between theoretical project management concepts and real-world business needs through energetic and engaging sessions.

In addition to the courseware, Belinda is the author of, *Kick Ass Project Manager*, a practical and straight-forward approach to tackling challenging projects. Belinda partners with leading HR and OD experts in the upcoming release of *You@Work*, an anthology focused on unleashing potential. In addition, her soon-to-be released book, *SHIFT: Business Growth through Exceptional Project Management* is already receiving positive reviews.

While she will always consider herself a die-hard Mainiac (Mainer), Belinda escaped the cold and relocated to Arizona where she currently resides. She has three daughters, including two who proudly served in the U.S. Navy, and six grandchildren. In her rare spare time, Belinda enjoys genealogy research as a Mayflower Descendant and Daughter of the American Revolution. Her next book is historical non-fiction about her fifth great-grandmother, Elizabeth Goodrich, a pioneer during the American Revolution. Belinda is currently pursuing her Ph.D. in Industrial and Organizational Psychology.

Interested in learning more about Belinda?

- Email: Belinda@PMLearningSolutions.com
- Facebook: www.facebook.com/PMBelindaSpeaks/
- Twitter: @PMBelindaSpeaks
- Linkedin: www.linkedin.com/in/belindagoodrich/
- www.PMLearningSolutions.com
- www.BelindaGoodrich.com

CHAPTER 6

HOW A HEART ATTACK LED TO A DENTAL REVOLUTION

BY DR. NILO A. HERNANDEZ, Jr.

A couple of years back, my life changed in many ways. At the time, my dentistry career was thriving, and I was enjoying the everyday challenges that go with this career... and then it happened. The unthinkable: I was struck with chest pain.

I was taken to the hospital, where I was told I had experienced two "silent" heart attacks. To say I was shocked would be an understatement. I wasn't sure how to take the news; however, I had no choice but to accept it and hope for the best outcome.

Over a period of several days, I underwent various tests including some key genetic tests, and I was definitely not a happy camper when I got the final results: I was told I would forever be a cardiac patient. Upon my release, I wondered long and hard about whether everyone who goes through this ordeal feels the same way. Did all of them wonder, as I was wondering, whether I would live long enough to see my kids graduate medical school, whether I would live to see them give me grandchildren...or, hell, for that matter, would I even live long enough just see them grow up and accomplish life's goals?

Was everyone else in my position as obsessed with these thoughts as I was, I wondered. And "obsessed" was probably quite the correct word, as these thoughts and others of that ilk controlled my every waking hour over the following days. But as the sole provider in our household, I had to get up, go out, make a living, and persevere. And so, persevere I did.

One early Thursday morning, I told my wife I was going to reinvent myself on the other Florida coast, where life is a bit slower and much more serene. I told her my plan: I would stake out temporary residence at a hotel and then secure a dental job. With my special skillset and knowledge on dental implants, I felt sure that finding a position would not be difficult.

The cardiac report on me was lengthy, detailed, and informative. As I read over the many pages, I found myself intrigued by how much real and solid information it contained about me and about how I was put together. I was very impressed. I dug around online, curious to find out as much as I could about some of those very specific tests. The report stated that I should get checked out by my dentist to make sure I did not have periodontal disease. Ironic, yes? It brought me to a realization, however, that for a few years I had been using a genetic laboratory for the differential diagnosis of periodontal disease. I had sparingly used this company to treat only those very difficult cases in which the patients bounced around from dentist to dentist with no variance in the results. And it hit me: I had been totally missing the boat.

My "aha moment" came as I began to truly appreciate the value of these tests. They should be discussed and recognized in the mainstream media for their value and the information they conveyed. For a mere 300 dollars and a simple saliva rinse done in the office, it is incredible the amount of valuable information I will receive in a week or so. The reports they send are detailed, full of informative content related to the one specific person and no one else… the one I just tested. The interpretation is also quite easily understood. They explain everything in fine detail and simple language. The levels of bacteria are clearly shown with the markers of the body's tolerance to those attacking bacteria. The genetic company has a few other tests that I also find useful from time to time like for instance their HPV test. That is an area getting much attention these days, especially among younger people.

You see, for years I had helped patients get their smiles back. I had helped them get their ability to chew back. But occasionally some patient who should have had standard results simply did not. Whenever that happened, the case kept me up at night, sleepless, pondering what the issue was and how to resolve it. So, I decided, in a few of these cases, to do these tests myself, and at my own cost, no less, to determine if there was an underlying reason for the failure to achieve good results. Was there something I had missed, some factor I was unaware of, or had I simply blown it?

What I was able to find out was mind-blowing.

These tests helped me identify the top really bad bacteria in the body of each of these patients. They also allowed me to determine their bodies' ability to handle inflammation, and the threshold levels at which the patient's body can tolerate these offending genetic markers.

The more I delved into this topic, the more I became aware that the second leading cause of cardiovascular incidents and stroke was periodontal disease. This was incredible evidence that, on certain patients, it did have a marked impact on how they handled disease and the corrective therapies.

So, off I went again on my discovery cruise along the knowledge highway called the internet. I researched high and low for these markers and what they meant to the body and how it related to what I was doing for patients. Now, after all these years of placing and restoring dental implants and helping countless thousands of patients achieve a winning smile, I was on to something special.

I knew up front how to detect their own pitfalls and how to synchronize my treatments to better serve them and have a much more favorable outcome.

A few patients truly surprised me. These were the people who showed up for a follow-up visit only to advise me that the information on the genetic tests I had given them was so impactful that they had shown it to their medical doctors or cardiologists. Some of those doctors even called me to discuss how I obtained this information. They were shocked that I was a dentist and was looking deeper into their patients' bodies than they were. I remember one doctor jokingly ask me if I was a frustrated cardiologist. I laughed him off but did answer that I was a frustrated healer of people.

Meanwhile, my dental life continued. Patients from all walks of life would come in for an in-depth study regarding their mouths, their problems, and their options, whether it involved a single tooth or an entire mouth. I found myself more involved than before in what their family history revealed and what the current state of their health was. I realized this was vital information that I needed before looking into their options for a new smile or new mouth. This new avenue brought about a renewed sense of my dental practice and what I could accomplish with it. It has reinvigorated me to help even more people to achieve what they have wanted for many years.

Dental implants are considered to be the gold standard of tooth replacement. A long-standing track record of dental implants proves them to be the best-functioning, best-looking, and best-feeling of all the tooth replacement options ever created by man. The national success ratio is over 95 percent. But for the few who have a failure, the failure rate is ultimately 100 percent, and that was something I could not handle very easily. There had to be a better answer.

By combining state-of-the-art medicine and genetic sciences, we are now able to predict with more confidence whether a person will fall into the successful category or not. And with this knowledge, we are now able to put the brakes on the occurrence of such pitfalls by redesigning what we do and how we do it based on science and not just mechanics. Dentistry has long been about the mechanics: Dentists see a hole and fill it, never once asking themselves: "Why did this break?" The answer may, in fact, lie not in the mouth but in the body and in the patient's personal DNA makeup.

Over the past couple of years, I have been using this information to create long-lasting, beautiful mouths that warrant and merit the expense and the life-altering improvements that come with them. Dental implants are screws. They are placed within the jawbone to secure a crown or a bridge with teeth in any number of ways. This mechanical phenomenon gives patients the ability to speak and chew proudly and without fear of having their dentures fall out. A person's life is incomplete when they are missing teeth or can't smile and chew. But, my life's purpose is to fulfill giving back those abilities to people. Making them whole again and giving someone the self confidence of speaking, chewing, smiling, eating and all the things that come with our own teeth and what those teeth provide.

The many benefits of dental implants stem from the mere fact that the bone cells themselves should and could tie up to the implant body and create a type of bear hug, and those same cells are predicted to impregnate themselves into the roughened surface of the implant. The stronger and more capable the blood cells are, the better that connection is. If we know how the body is built beforehand and what can be done prior to treatment to fortify and cleanse the body of the bad bacteria, then we can assume a better outcome later.

Imagine a race car with good, clean fuel versus one with dirty fuel and weakened structure. The weaker of the two will probably break down earlier than the better one. It might even break down during the race. The role of our genetic profile plays a very important part in our overall longevity and how we age. Periodontal disease is the second leading cause of some (non-dental) illnesses that fully break down the body. In addition, periodontal disease is the leading cause of tooth loss. Studies show that people missing even one tooth will live a lifespan approximately ten years shorter than those not missing any teeth. Why … you ask? Well, nutrition is fuel. The ability or inability to chew certain foods will have an impact. Digestion starts in the oral cavity, and mixing foods properly with saliva and the components within that saliva starts the process of breaking down foods to extract those gems of nutritional value.

Denture wearers are a special type of sick body. They can't chew—and this is true even in those whose dentures fit relatively well. The fact is that denture teeth are softer, in addition to which the denture base compresses against the underlying gums. These facts are enough to cause dentures to be notably less efficient in chewing than natural teeth. Denture wearers puzzled me for many years. I would see patients who appeared self-conscious about their looks, who had successful jobs and family lives. Yet they wore dentures for many years and thought that was normal since Mom or Grandma had them.

Medical and dental offices have their routine forms, the kind we all roll our eyes at having to fill out every time we go to see any doctor. But a form that is notably missing in many offices, yet should not be, is the family history form. It may reveal very important facts that will lead us to a better diagnosis and plan for an eventual successful outcome. I refer to this as my "crystal ball dentistry" approach.

What I will routinely do now is have new patients fill out a form based solely on their immediate past family tree. Are these family members still alive? Have any of them passed on? What illnesses did they have or succumb to? At what age did they get diagnosed with these illnesses? You might be surprised to find out how few people actually know these answers. I need them and will ask them to retrieve the information for me. This is not about being different. It's about being better able to help the patients to a more satisfactory outcome.

When patients understand this need, they will understand why they have had the failures they had in the past. We all know someone who heals fast from a simple cut, as well as people who take forever and a day to heal from the same type of cut. Ever wonder and ask yourself why? The answers lie in the genetic makeup. There are inflammatory markers that define who we are and how we handle these types of attacks on our bodies.

Nowadays when I see my daily roster of patients asking me for an implant or telling me that they just want teeth in a day, such as they saw on television, I stop and ask them what led them to arrive at this point. Usually the question throws them off at first. But as we embark on my quest for information, they soon realize that I am unlike any other dentist they have ever sat across from. They feel at ease and also feel that someone finally cares about them and why they have fallen to this point. I use surveys to ask patients their opinions and to relay the experiences they felt with me and my approach. The responses have been overwhelmingly positive, and this is just the beginning.

This essay will open your eyes much as it opened mine. Ask yourself these questions and finish them by asking yourself why did this happen to you?

- ❖ Are you on medications?
- ❖ Do you have diabetes or a heart condition?
- ❖ Have you had any teeth removed or ever been told to have them removed?
- ❖ Do you have periodontal (gum) disease?

The answers to these questions will help you live a better and more profound life.

I conclude by saying that I feel an obligation to pursue the best and available options to help patients and people of all walks of life live better, more healthy lives and enjoy the happiness that comes with one of God's greatest gifts to us all… our smiles.

About Dr. Nilo

Nilo A. Hernandez Jr., DDS, DICOI completed his dental degree at Creighton University, Omaha, Nebraska in 1991. Prior to that, he also completed dental training overseas that placed much emphasis on surgery and trauma procedures. With so much training in the surgical arts, it's no wonder that he has excelled on this chosen path with the greatest of passion and vigor.

Since 1991, Dr. Hernandez has placed and restored well over 10,000 dental implants and has achieved and maintained an extremely high success rate. Not only is he involved with the surgical aspect, but he has always been involved with the restorative side as well. For many years, he has been teaching dentists to become extraordinary with predictable results. As program chairman at two illustrious dental teaching clinics, he was instrumental in bringing Implant Dentistry to the mainstream at those centers and still is to this day. He has published numerous articles, books and been featured in many television and radio shows.

While being fluent in English and Spanish, he has lectured worldwide and given many thousands of hours of lectures on everything from surgical to prosthetic rehabilitation. He has impacted the lives of many dentists and patients from across the globe.

Teaching

The teaching arm has been developed due to his abilities and comprehensive use of methods, techniques and materials followed by proper and concise documentation and photography to assist many companies in using Dr. Hernandez' skills for research and development of their products.

As Course Director for the IDEC Seminar series, his quest is to prepare clinicians to reach levels of aptitude and proficiency never reached before. In addition to this, the medical advances in stem cells and genetic testing has become a part of the everyday dental practice life for Dr. Hernandez.

The skillsets that set Dr. Nilo apart from his competitors are:

- His dedication and striving for excellence at every chance
- A reputation based on excellence by choice, to deliver the highest performance
- He has achieved the highest accolades and awards in the dental profession
- He delivers a highly personal approach to patient care with extreme attention to detail

Personal

He has a wife and 2 wonderful children who also enjoy water activities and sunshine. Boating, soccer and photography are his hobbies.

To contact Dr. Hernandez:

- Tel: (239) 692-7511
- Email: nilodentist@gmail.com

CHAPTER 7

THE FIVE SECRET WEAPONS

BY VIKTORIA RINGHAUSEN

With the will to win and the desire to succeed,
you will be unstoppable!

It was a freezing cold night. The wind was so harsh it fought me and slapped me on the face like sharp needles. My routine walk to and from work was only twenty minutes, but during winter, that felt like an eternity.

One night, I noticed a figure walking close behind me. I turned around to see a large man, stumbling drunk. My survival instinct kicked in, and I ran without looking back. I was so frightened. I clutched two bags of freshly baked bread that I had to bring home. You see, I had people depending on me.

When I finally reached my building, I was unharmed but still terrified. My heart pounded in my chest as I fumbled for my keys. The dirty, dark hallway of the building where I lived smelled of urine, which was not new. At that moment, I remember feeling so much anger: anger at my life, my mom and my stepfather. I wanted to blame everyone for my misfortune. But then I had a liberating thought – one that changed my path and brought me to writing this to you today. In my despair, I realized I had nothing … and this was freeing! For me, there was nowhere to go but up. It was from this place of struggle that I came upon a path for my success: what I now call my "secret weapons."

Secret Weapon #1: When you have nothing, you have nothing to lose and everything to gain.

I was born and raised in Russia. Russia is tough; it is a land of extremes. You are always in survival mode. This mentality is handed down from generation to generation. When the Soviet Union collapsed, I was fifteen, a teenager trying to find my own voice. With all the changes happening around me, I realized that there were other possibilities I hadn't ever considered.

All of the pop culture and media that was forbidden before the fall of the Soviet Union flooded into our towns. We suddenly had access to TV and films such as Pretty Woman and Fight Club. We danced to Michael Jackson and Pink Floyd. We were all dizzy from the feeling of freedom and excitement, and curious about what was to come. For the first time in my life, I didn't feel stuck; I was open to new ideas and possibilities. All my dreams were possible … just not where I was living. The reality was that, in Russia, there were no jobs or opportunities without knowing someone. I didn't have those connections. You see, before the collapse, my life was already predestined: a guaranteed job, marriage, children. You could say that my predictable future crumbled with the collapse of the Soviet Union.

Even during these trying times, somehow I knew there was more for me. I had a big imagination, and in many ways my hardships freed me to hope and dream bigger.

I was young, but old enough to work. So, when someone offered me work at the small, local bakery, I jumped at the chance. What did I have to lose?

Secret Weapon #2: Grab every opportunity that comes your way.

Back in those days, I worked nights at the bakery, took mechanical engineering classes in the evening, and slept during the day. I said 'yes' to everything I could because I could not pass up any possibility or opportunity. On those miserable winter evenings, it was a blessing to come to the warm bakery with the wonderful smell of freshly-baked bread. I felt lucky and grateful. Which brings me to my next lesson.

Secret Weapon #3: Always be grateful for the opportunity.

There is a quote I think of often by William Arthur Ward: "Gratitude can transform common days into thanksgivings, turn routine jobs into joy and change ordinary opportunity into blessing." Gratitude is key to appreciating what you have, even when (especially when) it is very little.

This secret weapon truly helped me persevere during tough times. We were very poor. However, I remember feeling so blessed that I could bring bread to my neighbor's kids and my friends. I noticed that our gratitude kept our heads up: we appreciated the little things, and our eyes were open for when the next good thing might come along.

One practice I recommend to others is showing your appreciation every chance you have. Take the time to give thanks for what you have, and the opportunities you've been granted. Show your appreciation by telling a friend or neighbor "thank you," even for a simple gesture. If you can work this into your daily life, you will find great rewards (including, often, more opportunities!).

Back in Russia when I had a rare day off from the bakery, I used to go to the boardwalk to watch the cruise ships dock. They were so glamorous! They represented something unattainable and in motion, something exciting. I would close my eyes and imagine walking along the red carpet, coming down the stairs and smiling at the tourists, sitting down at the restaurant with a glass of champagne and dessert in front of me. God, I could even smell the food! What a perfect life! Right? The fantasy was so real for me.

I am a strong believer in the Law of Attraction, the philosophy that we attract whatever we are focused on into our lives. Of course, I didn't know anything about it then, but I remember the feeling I had. Wouldn't you know that somehow, two years later, I was on that cruise ship! I got a job on board as a dishwasher. Well, what else could I do? I did not speak English at that time, and you must speak a little English to communicate with the tourists. I knew my limitations, but I also saw it as a foot in the door, so to speak. I would continue to work hard (Secret Weapon #2) and appreciate what I had been granted (Secret Weapon #3).

Aboard the cruise ship of my dreams, the reality was that I wanted to move out of the kitchen washing dishes and become a waitress. I wanted to learn English. I remember one night, cleaning up after a party on board, I found myself looking out at the sea wondering about my destiny. Which leads me to Secret Weapon #4.

Secret Weapon #4: Ask Like a Child.

If you have children, you know exactly what I mean. The other day, my four-year-old son came to me and asked, "Mom, can I have ice cream for breakfast?" I said no. After three more attempts, I finally gave in to his tenacity. Apparently, he learned it from his mother! Deciding when is the right time to ask is a skill we can develop as adults. Sometimes, we have to engage our inner child and ask more than once to get what our heart truly wants.

Back on my cruise ship, I knew I wanted things to change. I bravely decided to go to the banquet hall manager to ask if I could become a waitress.

"Do you speak English?" she asked.

"No."

"Well, then the answer is *no*."

However, I had nothing to lose. I was determined, armed with my Secret Weapons, I continued washing dishes and keeping an eye on the banquet hall. When two waitresses quit, I returned to her with the same question. Again, she asked, "Do you speak English?"

"A bit," I said. (I was learning.) Once again, she said no.

As fate would have it, two more waitresses quit. I returned again with the same question. She looked at me and sighed.

"Okay, fine. But if you mess up, you will go back to be the dishwasher."

Life on a cruise ship is tough and frantic, but if you survive you make amazing friends for life. All of us work five months straight: seven days a week, with 10 to 16-hour shifts every single day! Every year I swore it was my last year, and every year I returned...for five years. There is something fulfilling about working so hard, but there is little time for much else. And while I enjoyed it to a large extent, questions plagued me. "What is my destiny? What is my purpose? There must be something more."

My last year on the cruise ship is when I met my husband. He was a tourist aboard the ship: a young, handsome boy from America. He was like from another planet – so different from anyone I knew. Our love story lasted for ten days at sea. After he left, everyone (including me!) assumed we would never see each other again. Despite all the odds, he came back and proposed.

Then my new journey began. We moved to the United States. I

still was struggling to learn English, and I had never learned how to drive. Everything and everyone was unfamiliar – exciting and scary all at the same time.

I was with the love of my life, full of happiness and gratitude. We were poor at the beginning, but compared to Russia, we were rich! We had a large apartment, a car, a microwave, washer, and dryer. I ate bean and bacon soup every other day, and I didn't have to wait for a special holiday to eat chicken. It was a truly blessed time, and I was surrounded by kind people and opportunities. I remember telling myself when I had self- doubt that I had nothing to lose (Secret Weapon #1) and to keep my head up.

My first job in America was at the Kroger deli, walking distance from our home. I was so grateful to be given a chance. I learned how to decorate cakes, continued learning English, as well as how to drive a car. In time, I was teaching cake decorating classes and English as a second language at the local library. My life kept moving me forward because I was determined, and open to opportunities as they arose.

Looking back on it now, it seems like it all happened so quickly. But in those five years, I kept taking small steps forward. Sometimes, I got discouraged and thought I would never be able to accomplish anything. My husband was still a student; we moved several times for his schooling. Each time, we had to start from ground zero: find a job, make new friends, and build a life. I loved the excitement of moving to new places, but I was not happy with myself or the jobs I ended up taking. The worst part was that I lost my drive. As a result, my husband and I barely talked. I was angry all the time, mainly for feeling like I had sacrificed my life to follow him.

Then I made the classic mistake of thinking that if I had a baby, all of life's problems would go away. As it turns out, I was unable to get pregnant for five years. We tried everything, it was devastating. But looking back, I am so grateful: a baby cannot save a broken person or a relationship. Sometimes things truly do (or don't!) happen for a reason.

It was around this time that I came across the book, *The Secret*. It was like a wake-up call. I had these questions again burning me inside, "What is my destiny? What is my purpose? There has to be something more than this." It fueled me to reignite my passion and find my 'will to win' again.

I believe sometimes it is good to get angry with yourself. Life is short. Nobody knows how many days they have left to live. If you are not happy, you must do something about it. Take responsibility and stop blaming others. Change your course. Remember your secret weapons and employ them!

I was working as a waitress when one of my regulars left me a letter with an exciting opportunity he thought I'd be a great fit for. It had information about real estate classes. This felt like a sign from the universe, and the timing could not have been better. I signed up to attend.

Real estate is already extremely competitive – and it gets even more challenging when you are new to the industry and have a thick Russian accent. One piece of advice I got from the broker was to lose my accent if I wanted to be successful (easier said than done!). But a 'will to win' is a powerful force. I persevered because it was important to me.

I believe in taking my chances, staying positive, and being grateful for every opportunity. I also have discovered a true calling for helping and inspiring others. While reading motivational kinds of literature, I discovered amazing teachers like Brian Tracy, Jack Canfield, Napoleon Hill, Les Brown, and Bob Proctor. Today, I consider all of them my mentors. I am grateful for their insights and contributions, because they have brought me to yet another exciting chapter in my life.

<u>Secret Weapon #5:</u> Keep yourself motivated.

My will to win and the desire to make a difference motivates me constantly. This outlook complements my work in real estate and has illuminated another true calling: helping people.

Every morning, I read inspiring stories and listen to motivational speeches. I call this "exercise for the mind." These empowering texts help me feel more confident, and give me the insight I bring into a new day. But nothing happens by accident. You must make a habit of setting intentions and creating routines that strengthen you and help you focus on the things that you are meant to do. Only then can positive things happen; only then can you begin to attract amazing opportunities and the right people.

I was very fortunate to work with a builder who took a chance on me – he would later become my mentor. He coached me, and now I have a successful real estate career that I absolutely love. Life is great! I have two beautiful children, a loving, supportive husband and close friends.

But still the questions remain: "Is this my destiny? Is this my purpose? I know I can do more than this."

Women frequently tell me that my story has inspired them to go after their dream. Folk-singer Ani Difranco wrote, "every tool is a weapon, if you hold it right." I have come to believe that my secret weapons carried me towards success and better circumstances. I also believe that others can pull from their own special strengths and develop the arsenal they need to win at life.

That is why I want to share my ideas with you. I want to empower you to identify your secret weapons and employ them to get whatever you most desire. It is my sincere hope that you can say yes to opportunities and believe that anything is possible. To do so, you must take action to create the life you were meant to live. But you don't need to have it all figured out to start. Just start today with one little step.

What do you have to lose? If you don't ask, the answer is always no.

But what if you *do* …

About Viktoria

Viktoria Ringhausen believes that when you have the will to win, and the desire to succeed, you are unstoppable. Born in Russia, Viktoria overcame great odds to become a successful author, speaker, coach, and real estate advisor.

With a strong will to win and an eye for opportunity, Viktoria landed a position on a cruise ship that turned into a golden ticket to the United States. She describes her job as a dishwasher on a cruise ship as a character-building experience that taught her how to always ask for more. She sees opportunities everywhere! Beyond a keen sense of command in her real estate business, Viktoria coaches others, so they too can experience success in business and more importantly, in life. She is a certified Jack Canfield trainer in Success Principles, and a certified Les Brown Maximum Achievement trainer.

Viktoria's college degree is in mechanical engineering, and that has served her well in mastering real estate and home construction. She is a high performing, licensed Realtor® in the state of Maryland.

One of her life's favorite stories, however, happened on the cruise ship, where she met her husband. She lives in Maryland with her husband and two beautiful young children.

To contact Viktoria Ringhausen, please go to:
- www.FindtheWilltoWin.com

CHAPTER 8

LESSONS THAT GRIEF TAUGHT ME ABOUT LIFE

BY DONNA-LEE GREAVES

Life is fleeting and precious. Everyone knows that, though few may assimilate its impact; the true core of its meaning. You can't buy the experience of the love that you receive from the significant people in your life. Those that affect, and have an effect, on you. Stuff can't hold you and comfort you. It won't belly laugh with you, and it certainly won't cry with you when you're sad. It's just stuff! It will not ever be a substitute for the people whom you have loved and lost, those who loved you.

Grief is full of surprises. So often when you think you are doing fine, it will find a way to slap you back to reality. You have lost someone (I'd say something, but pets are people, too), and grief isn't likely to let you forget that in a hurry.

There are so many things that no one ever tells you about grief and loss, though; before you lose someone, or even after. For instance, you never hear, "It's okay to laugh, if that's what you feel like." The one that you lost will be gladdened by it, not disappointed that you're having fun. It is not for others, either, to judge you by your happiness or tears. How much, how little, how long. They will only judge you because they know no better.

Forgive them, they are ignorant or inexperienced in grief and may even fear their own feelings or reactions.

All emotional reactions – crying, laughter, sobbing, smiling, reflecting – are natural expressions of a healthy soul. Suppression – like the typically British stiff-upper-lip of my ancestors – does not EVER make a soul healthy. Let alone maintain the health and wellness of the body that contains it. A healthy, wholehearted expression of grief is necessary for the ongoing wellness of the body.

It has been said that resilience is the key to a long and happy life, and there is no denial that this is important. It has been my experience, though, that resilience cannot come until after the feelings of grief have been felt, acknowledged, assimilated and incorporated. The purpose of grief and loss in our lives – there must be one, or there would be no point – is for our personal growth. It is one of our greatest teachers about life, ourselves and others.

Grief can be very sneaky. Just when you think you've covered all the bases, it will sidle up to you from an unexpected angle. Today, 29th of September 2017, is the 26th National Police Remembrance Day, since my brother and his police motorcycle parted company. I could not bring myself to attend the service, as it would be my first alone since Mum passed away (some 15 years after my dad's passing). Instead, I went and sat with them (Tony, dad and mum), at the crematorium.

For two hours, I sat and communed with them, and wrote; the music of trucks thundering up the highway, my only accompaniment. Nought but one distraction: my partner blasting his airhorn as he passed by – twice, as if I'd missed the first – to let me know that he was thinking of me; with me in heart and spirit. At the thought of still being loved, I cleaned the vase and added some colourful flowers for them to enjoy, shared my apple with the insistent magpies (no doubt sent by mum) and watched the changing light on the "family rock", as the sun rose behind me.

It was a lovely, peaceful way of acknowledging the day, in quiet, solitary contemplation. Not for show, in front of the Police Service hierarchy, politicians and other dignitaries; nor the watchful eye of the media, ever keen for a story of pain.

Last year, I'd told mum that I thought enough was enough, no more depressing services. She had become more frail by the year. Annually, I wondered if this would be the year that she would collapse laying memorial flowers, and that I would have to pick her up. In a brief attack of the guilts, I thought that I should attend once more, in her honour. I'm very glad that I chose otherwise.

For me, the day was always going to be sad, so it was a simple matter of choosing the best way to spend it, for my own personal growth. Not a day to express my leadership, I did that last year when we walked up to lay the flowers. I stepped right to the middle of the "official" floral tributes, parted them, placing ours front and centre.

My brother gave his life riding a motorcycle that was deemed unsafe by the coroner, while answering a call to escort an ambulance, on a mercy dash. He did not deserve to be forgotten, nor treated as inconsequential. In saying this – owning my feelings – it is me that feels like this, not he.

Though the senior officers would invite my mother and greet her after the services, I may as well have been invisible. My own grief and loss were never acknowledged. This baby brother of mine – my only sibling – who had been in my life for 26 years. We had been a double act at many a gathering, rendering our friends into fits of laughter, as we verbally bounced off each other. Where so many siblings seem to bicker, we were always each other's best friend and confidant.

When I was told of his passing, it felt as if someone had torn into my chest and ripped out half of my heart. The pain was that tangible. It is an ache that has dulled with time yet was so different to the passing of my parents, or the miscarriage that I suffered some two and half years after his death. Every grief, for every individual person, every time, is different. For those that are unable to learn and grow, each new grief gets piled onto the previous one, until the burden of hurt is overwhelmingly unbearable.

The alternative is to face each grief with courage and compassion for yourself. Feel your emotions as you need to, when you need to. Remain in the moment. When you need to cry, do it then. It's a primal urge, like going to the toilet. You don't necessarily want to do it in front of other people, but you can't keep putting it off until later. Taking drugs to numb the pain is akin to having no fibre in your diet. Eventually you are going to have to change things, and the pain is likely to get worse before it gets better.

As difficult as it may be, the Universe/God, or [insert your alternative here] would not have given you this to deal with, if you didn't have the capacity to cope. You are far stronger than you realise, and capable of great acts of bravery, if only you would step up to the plate. Your potential for resilience is more powerful than you can comprehend. Be kind to yourself, and fold into your grief, as you would bend into a strong wind.

Acknowledge your past difficulties. You have learned so much since you took that courageous first breath into this life. Didn't you learn to ride your bicycle without training wheels, go to school by yourself, go out on your first date? What firsts of your own did you conquer? If you don't believe me, right them down and keep adding to your list, as you face them.

Things to help you grow through your grief, drawn from my experiences:

- **Feel into your grief without delay.** These feelings may be new to you, and to those around you.

- **Understand there are phases of grief.** The concept of these five steps was first purported in Elisabeth Kübler-Ross's 1969 book, *On Death and Dying*. Learning about these in the months following my brother's death helped me immeasurably; to understand this process so new to me, as well as most of my supportive friends. The time that you spend in each stage will vary, and sometimes you will feel like you have dropped back a step or two, before you can progress.

Briefly the steps are:

- **Denial** – feelings of pain (physical and/or emotional) and numbness, sense of the surreal (as if you are an observer); thoughts like "What has happened?", "This can't be true!" or "They are too young."

- **Anger** – may be directed at yourself, at whomever you've lost, at family/friends, and even at the World. This can be a particularly intense period, which may be very draining, energetically. Maintaining this state for too long can also be quite unhealthy; I watched my mum stuck in this for about a year, while she fought for a Coroner's inquest, following my brother's crash.

- **Bargaining** – there can be an element of guilt in this phase, with a desire to somehow have that time over. You may insist "What could I have done/said?" or "If only we'd had one last hug.", none of which can ever bring them back to you.

- **Depression** – thoughts of great sadness for the future, in the absence of your dear one. It can feel like a very deep, dark hole, and sometimes when you think that you could not possibly go any deeper, you do. This is the time when you need to feel into it more, not less. Call in your best support here, your friends or your counsellor.

- **Acceptance** – altogether now: "Sigh!" You've made it, though it was not easy. You will never be the same person again, but that is a good thing. When you make it this far, you will realise that you have become a more grateful, compassionate human being. Now you are ready to enjoy life, again.

For more detail, the website of Kübler-Ross's co-author, David Kessler, is worth investigating.[1]

- Deal with each loss as it arises. Putting it off until things get better can make everything so much harder to cope with.

- Be kind to yourself, and others. This is a time to have great compassion for yourself and others. In fact, this is an excellent way to live your life, at any time. Think before you speak – or write, on social media – you can never know what another person is facing, how they are dealing with something or what experiences have led them to where they're at, right now.

- Feed yourself good, nutritious food. This may sound obvious, but it is too easy to neglect yourself when you are grieving, then you may become rundown. Be prepared to nurture yourself – or allow others to – making a conscious effort to prepare healthy, delicious meals is a way of honouring those that you have lost; with gratitude for their love.

- You might feel like you need to cry, but you don't know how. You want to release the pressure of your hurt. Talking about your loss with an understanding friend or counsellor

---

1. https://grief.com/the-five-stages-of-grief/

can help. Even simply watching a touching movie – such as *Beaches, The Green Mile, Life is Beautiful* or *Bridge to Terabithia* – can pull on your heart-strings enough to open the floodgate of stored tears.

It may not even be a movie known for being sad or tragic. Shortly after my dad's passing, I watched *Love Actually* and laughed heartily, until the closing scene, where people are reuniting in airports. This rendered me into deep, audible sobs (thankfully the packed cinema was still in darkness), this had been the experience of me with my dad. Since the early 80s he would regularly fly in and out of Brisbane airport, near my home. A simple reminder of those times of deep connection.

- Milestones will come – birthdays (yours, theirs), Mother's or Father's Day – and they will be tough. Even years down the track, when you think you are over it, on a bad day you suddenly notice the date. Your body remembers, even if your mind is too busy.

- Last of all, remember this: You were born with the will to win. It is, after all, the reason that you chose to incarnate. Allow yourself to collapse into the natural grieving process. In your own way and in your own time, not on someone else's timetable.

About Donna-Lee

Donna-Lee is an author and highly intuitive remedial massage therapist. She has focused her life and career in the regional city of Maryborough, Queensland, after many years of living and working in Brisbane.

Her passion and expertise lie in natural medicine, rehabilitation and sports medicine. Her long-held interest in sports and natural medicine stemmed from a family passion for healing. Many of her skills were learned when she was a teenager, from her chiropractor/naturopath father: a man well known for his healing abilities in the Maryborough sporting community.

She understands the deep connection between body and soul, having experienced the effects of grief on the body from when she lost her brother and only sibling at the age of 28. At 55, she is now the only surviving member of her family: both parents and other family members also transitioning. Growing up in the bush was quite isolating and resulted in a closeness within the family. This made the pain of losing them all the more intense.

These losses caused her to go deep within herself to reflect on life, clearing blockages and understanding the lessons behind all of it. Her coping mechanism was simple: she cried when she needed to cry and laughed when she needed to laugh, even when this made other people uncomfortable.

Donna-Lee knows the healing power of words, as well as touch. By healing herself it has taught her to find the right things to say to heal others. Through writing, facilitating and teaching, she combines her bodywork skills with lightwork. Utilising intuitive abilities, she witnesses results at a deep level for those who are struggling with grief, pain or other personal challenges.

The lure of healing and helping others has always been strong, driving her to continually build knowledge and skills to allow better assistance to clients, in health and wellbeing challenges. Donna-Lee has recently upgraded her massage qualifications to allow a more comprehensive service to her clients. While understanding the importance of appropriate qualifications, she has augmented this formal education with a commitment to learn from those around her.

Donna-Lee is a committed member of her community, constantly contributing to the building of community spirit and looking for new ways to offer service. For many years, she has been passionately involved with the Fraser Coast Technology Challenge, which sees thousands of participants descending on Maryborough every September. Donna-Lee has also given back to her old school, Maryborough State High, through active contribution to the school's Parents and Citizens Association.

Donna-Lee has begun focusing her energy into one of the key nutrients for all living beings – WATER: as pure and alive as nature intended it. A scientist by degree, holding a Bachelor of Human Movement Science, and by nature, accessing the best quality water for herself, her family and her clients is deeply satisfying and ultimately rewarding for her. She continues to research the best methods of healing and products for health.

You can connect with Donna-Lee at:

- www.jalahm.com.au

CHAPTER 9

TO WIN THE RACE, YOU CANNOT QUIT!

BY SULEIMAN SHAIBU

Grey clouds put a blanket in the sky, in time for the cool evening breeze. This weather pattern had been consistent for five days. I am not a *weather man*. Not in the least. I don't even go by the predictions of a meteorologist, but I became more aware of my environment as I counted down to February 10, 2018. It was the night before the most crucial race of my life. In my trembling hands was a checklist of essentials for the Access Bank Lagos City Marathon. As I ticked off my list, I remembered the countenance of fear, doubt and disbelief on the faces of everyone that cared to listen to my bucket list ambition. Not one of them believed I could make it beyond 10km. (Who would blame them? At the time of the race, I weighed 97kg or (213.8 pounds). I was quick to counter their pessimism by proudly informing them of my milestone record two years earlier. I made it to 39.5km just before pulling a hamstring and could not run anymore.

The nerves became stronger, but it was too late to back out. I was afraid, scared of losing, not making it to 10km or running out of strength too early in the race. The voices of doubt echoed louder and louder as I began to reason out loud. "It's only a personal achievement. Perhaps, not as important as I thought.

I can replace this wish to run a second time with another one. Maybe a more respectable one that my friends can be proud of." I thought about all the Guinness Book of Records achievements I had read about. Sadly, none was as exciting as running with the possibility of winning the gold medal for the male category this time. Abraham Kiptum, a Kenyan, won it last year in a record time of 2 hours 15 minutes and 23 seconds.

So, on the 10th of February 2018, after 7 hours 30 minutes of grueling running and walking, I completed one of my bucket list items. Well, I decided running was not about my family or friends but rather my claim to personal victory. It was my marathon story and I did it because I wanted to win. Maybe not win literally but I had a desire to win. The desire to win was the fuel I needed, the impetus to hit a greater record than I did two years ago. I earned my bragging rights.

All humans are created equal. However, I think inequality comes as a result of our individual urge to accomplish something worthwhile or to give ourselves to a bigger cause or a greater goal. We all want to win. Yes, there is a natural inclination in all humans to triumph. However, it is important to accept the reality that success comes at a price. My example of running the marathon for a second time is probably not the best one you have read as I am not a professional athlete. So, I'll share a remarkable story to reiterate my point.

Paula Radcliffe is a renowned and knighted (MBE) British female long distance runner and a three times London and New York Marathon winner. On August 22, 2004 she represented Great Britain at the Athens Olympics. Thirty-six kilometers into the race (with just 8km left to finish), she had to quit due to a serious stomach upset. Apparently, the stomach discomfort was a side effect of an anti-inflammatory drug which she had taken for an injury she sustained two weeks before the race. Her fans were as devastated as she was. The press conference that followed was somber with a lot of crying and regrets. Five days later, she attempted a 10,000-meter race but also had to stop after running eight laps due to the same stomach upset. After such set backs, anyone would have called it quits, but not Paula Radcliffe.

The following year (2005), she participated in the 42km London Marathon. Around the 26km spot, she felt the call of nature and was left with no option than to stop to relieve herself. (Yes, you read that correctly; she stopped to poop before the crowd on national television.) Interestingly, she went on to win the race in record time of 2 hours 17 minutes and 42 seconds. In the same year, she won a medal for Britain at the world championship meet in Helsinki.

I am sharing this story because it underscores the driving force behind many people's success – which is the will to win.

The big question is, *"How badly do you want to win?"*

Success comes at a very high price. Sometimes the price paid affects our physical strength and health. Other times, we may need to sacrifice time and money. Time with friends and family is often affected while we spend lots of money to achieve the burning quest to win. Some people have propelled the will to win by negative motives and emotions which has led them to compromise their values, beliefs, and the love of their friends and family. Now, there is a healthy balance to this. My perspective is not in suggesting neglect. Not at all. However, it is impossible to realize monumental success without sacrificing time, money and energy. Something has to give. I think the greatest price you have to pay to be successful is the determination never to give up, no matter what.

As a professional, an entrepreneur and a business coach, I faced my litmus test seven years ago. July 22, 2012 was my first day at Microsoft as an employee. I had landed a job that many would have considered a dream one but with it came a mixture of emotions. I got to my desk to find a nicely wrapped gift with my name neatly written on it. I opened the package and to my delight, it contained a box of chocolates and a small note saying that it was great to have me on the team. It was one of the most beautiful welcome notes I had received on my first day at work. I was happy and sad at the same time. Why the sadness you would ask? For one, I was returning to paid employment having left ten years before. I recall telling one of the VPs in HP that visited Nigeria in 2002 that I was never going to return to paid employment, so you can imagine the embarrassment I felt, when I found myself back as an employee.

In the year 2002, I resigned from HP to start an IT business with some friends. With a dose of enthusiasm, hope and unwavering confidence about the future, I put in all our resources including my Jalopy Jetta car, and set sail to the land of entrepreneurship. I did not have much except the will to win. Bootstrapping was our only option because we did not have any funding from business angels, family or financial institutions. We were willing to take the risk. There was nothing to lose. I was not married, so I jumped in with both feet. We worked very hard on weekdays and weekends. We did not have a social life because we worked mostly nine to twelve hours daily (during the first few years, I did not take any vacation apart from the three days I took off for my honeymoon). This was our routine for many years before we started seeing significant results. At a time, we had eleven employees and hit the six-figure turnover.

In the fifth year of business as the CEO, I believed our business needed to move to the next level, so I enrolled for the Owner Manager's Program at the prestigious Lagos Business School. At the end of the six-month program, I informed my partners of my decision to part ways with them. I wanted to start a new company alone (we had several unresolved issues before then that had been lingering). I figured I could replicate my skills, hard work and experience in the partnership in my new company. It wasn't because I wanted to enjoy more success alone. I simply wanted to launch a different business without a partnership structure.

So, they bought me out. To my bewilderment, everything I did subsequently did not add up. I lost money, I lost all my investments and I could barely take care of my young family. I hit the proverbial brick wall. It was the most depressing season of my life. I could not take uncalculated risks because I was now responsible for a wife and two children. I had to do something. I had to succeed. I had to win.

At the age of 42, I was back in the labour market, despondent, only with a glimpse of hope, lacking confidence that I could pioneer a new business or achieve successful feats. You can imagine my fear and frustration. Who hires a tired, broken 42-year-old individual? Luckily, Microsoft still saw something in me. One of the executives, whom I met at the final stage of the interview, had a similar story to mine, so he could relate to my predicament.

Hence, the uneasiness on my first day at work. However, this faded away the longer I remained committed to learning and growing at my job. I soon noticed that there were many transferrable skills that could become very useful if I decided to go down the entrepreneurship path again, something I began to seriously consider. But I obviously needed to build more capacity and knowledge before venturing out on my own again, so I remained at Microsoft for a while before the lure into entrepreneurship again became irresistible to me. But those two and a half years there meant the world to me because they laid the foundation for much of the success I experienced in my next job and subsequent business adventure.

Here are my top lessons:

Microsoft expects high standards from her employees. The company trains and equips its staff to perform well on the job. They create that enabling environment for people who are focused and driven to excel in whatever they do. They challenge you to be the best that you can be and here is how:

1. **Quota Commitment:** Microsoft wants its people to take their quota commitment seriously. They do this through staff training, retreats and meetings. Everyone in the organization works tenaciously to meet and exceed their quota. They push hard till the very last day. The *never-say-die spirit* is truly worth emulating. Managers and executives get involved traveling and calling the sales team to offer their time and expertise to help close deals. *If you are a business owner, you need to keep pushing and inspiring your team by letting them know you are available to help win deals.*

2. **People Development:** They contribute to your career development plan by helping you improve continuously by increasing your knowledge and creating space for you to innovate within your role. Microsoft is confident of itself as an employer of choice. *As a business owner, it is important not to undermine the importance of training your staff – especially when comparing the benefits and opportunities that open up vis-a-vis the likelihood of employees leaving your organization after investing in their development.*

3. **Openness and Adaptability:** Did I tell you that one of my bosses was twelve years younger than I was? (It isn't a big deal now, although I was slightly conscious of the age gap back then.) My case was similar to the characters of Owen Wilson and Vince Vaughn in the movie – *The Internship.* I had to force myself to learn and re-learn new skills. *As a business owner, it is important to be open to receive new ideas and suggestions from your employees. They may introduce fresh perspectives and lead innovation that may improve your processes and bottom line.*

4. **All Round Development:** Microsoft advocates work-life balance. It wasn't until I joined Microsoft that I rekindled my interest in sports. I picked up playing table tennis and whilst doing so, I lost some weight. This lifestyle led to my bucket list ambition – running the marathon and finishing the race.

I was inspired by some of the managers and executives, they looked fit and dapper all the time. *As a business owner, you need to keep your health in close check. Don't be a couch potato, get a life and start exercising.*

5. **Embrace Change:** In 2013, it was becoming clear that Microsoft could not continue to sell its software purely on a straight one-time purchase or licensing method, so it embraced the cloud and rental business model. Changing their business model to accommodate market growth and demand has helped them remain relevant. *As a business owner, it is important to do a periodic analysis of your market. Remember, change is inevitable.*

6. **Feedback:** Feedback is the breakfast of champions. Microsoft cherishes feedback not only from staff but from its customers, which it conducts annually. The managers and divisions within the business Key Performance Indicator (KPI) are intertwined with the results and feedback gleaned from these customers. *As a business owner, what are you doing to get feedback from your customers on what you are doing right or wrong and what areas requires improvement?*

As a business coach, I interact with many budding entrepreneurs and business executives. They painstakingly create products and services all in a bid to launch the next big venture in their industry or become significantly profitable. Some of these executives and entrepreneurs attend annual retreats where they map out strategies whilst analyzing variances, reviewing their performance and thinking of new ways to do things better. They often hire consultants like me to facilitate these retreats with the hope that our recommended solutions, when implemented, will bring overall organizational growth – maximizing profit and reducing operational expenses. The common thread that runs through these entrepreneurs and business executives is their will to win.

I started out talking about my 'bucket list' ambition then I shared a little about how I transitioned from entrepreneur to employee and back to entrepreneur. My intention was to be a beacon of hope to someone reading this. I am hoping that my story will encourage you to forge ahead with your personal, business or corporate goal(s). Success is attainable when we clarify the objectives we want to achieve, becoming rugged in our determination to achieve these objectives, yet remaining flexible in our approach. Tony Robbins said, "Stay committed to your decisions, but stay flexible in your approach."

So, what price are you willing to pay to move your life, business or career to the next level?

About Suleiman

Suleiman Shaibu helps organizations and business executives find clarity in their business and personal development endeavors. His experience spans two decades during which he worked for leading multinational organizations like Hewlett Packard (HP), Microsoft and Temenos (Switzerland).

His interesting mixture of experiences in entrepreneurship have made him a resource person in great demand for entrepreneurs and business organizations. He co-pioneered a successful IT business and sold his majority stake in 2007 before starting BFT Consulting Services – which has given him opportunities to share his business experiences with leaders in different markets cutting across Nigeria, South Africa, Ghana, United Kingdom, USA and Canada.

Suleiman Shaibu has an Electrical Electronics Engineering Degree, and an MBA (specialty – International Marketing) from Federal University of Technology, Owerri, Imo State and ESUT Business School, Enugu State, Nigeria respectively.

Suleiman is a business consultant and leadership expert working with senior executives and businesses on their strategy, leadership and sales management challenges. He is a certified John Maxwell coach, trainer and speaker. He is also a certified Clarity4D UK trainer and coach. He has attended management programs at Harvard and Lagos Business Schools.

Suleiman is passionate about leadership and human development issues, especially those related to men. He is a sports enthusiast with special interests in table tennis, golf and running. He successfully completed the 2018 Lagos Access Bank Marathon.

Suleiman spends a lot of his time as a volunteer for social development projects. He is also one of the mentors for the African Entrepreneurship Award - 2018.

If you wish to reach out to get more information about his expertise, you can connect at:

- Suleiman@SuleimanShaibu.com
- http://will2win.SuleimanShaibu.com
- www.facebook.com/suleimanspeaks
- www.instagram.com/suleimanspeaks

CHAPTER 10

BE MENTALLY TOUGH TO WIN

BY JUDITH GLORY

The will to win has many times been associated with competitions. In general, the candidates demonstrating the greatest determination usually end up with the prize. Whether in a beauty, journalism, sports or art competition, the successful contenders habitually have a common trait that set them apart from the lot and qualifies them to be the gold holders: Mental toughness.

Also called grit, this is defined by Coach Vince Lombardi as "a perfectly disciplined state of mind that refuses to give in." Researcher David Yukelson defines it as a psychological edge that allows you to cope better than your competition with the demands that are placed on you, as well as the ability to perform consistently better than your competition.

A recent American survey shows that psychological traits are more important than physical characteristics in creating successful people. High levels of mental toughness are associated with athletic prowess and success. To some, it is considered the defining factor between the low and the great achievers.

So, let's take a closer look at what is mental toughness. It is characterized by:

Control:

This is the ability to own the responsibility for the results. Such athletes assume full responsibility for the outcome. They do not wait for the coach, the conditions or any other external factor to determine their fate. Even when the outcome is not the expected one, they fully take it upon themselves to understand why and to learn from any mistake or lack that could have been the cause of their performance.

Confidence:

Successful athletes believe in their capability to win. They know with absolute assurance that they have all it takes not only to take them among the best, but also that they are the best no matter who and how many other postulants were at the starting line.

Commitment:

The commitment and determination to win in tough contenders are extraordinarily high. Convinced that they have what it takes, the successful athletes do not joke about their training and preparation programme. They are willing to pay the price, do what it takes to develop their strengths, improve on their weak areas and put on new capacities to take them from one level to the ones above.

Consistency:

There is no way to have a serious contender who has no regular routine. Daily exercise forms the solid foundation used by the performer to develop his muscles, get out of his comfort zone, transform his body and thus be able to face a higher opponent and greater challenges.

Challenge:

If life was just about handling stuff in our comfort zone, most people would be able to make it. However, mentally tough individuals go beyond and accept facing giants, many times bigger, stronger, or more experienced than they are. The courage to oppose the unknown with the burning fire of unshakeable confidence qualifies them for the top.

Constructiveness:

Mentally tough people are also very positive, constructive individuals. When it happens that the outcome is not as expected – for example if they lose a battle – they do not stop, sit and wail, but instead, they use the failure as feedback to improve. As the saying goes, "Winners build on mistakes. Losers dwell on them." They fail forward.

Resiliency:

It is sure worth mentioning that for these high performers, the only options are to win or to win. They keep exercising and competing for as many times as required till they make it. Even if they fail one or more times, they try again and come back for the next session. Such insistence, perseverance, and resilience can only be explained by the fact that there are no two options for these candidates. They have set their mind to participate and win. If this means trying again and again and again, they are resilient and willing to do it.

Armed with such a determination, having no other option and committed to staying on it till the price is earned, no matter how long it would take and how much it would cost, the only outcome is to win.

** ** ** ** **

After some years in technology as an IT professional, Mory wanted to acquire the management insights that coupled with her experience, would make her a good IT manager. She wanted to earn a Master of Business Administration (MBA).

There was only one university offering the executive MBA program she needed. Each year, only fifty applicants were selected for admission. The tuition fee for the two-year program was sufficiently high to be, on its own, a selective barrier, leaving only a few financially capable professionals to compete for the seats.

To pay the cost for the first year of studies, Mory planned to use all her savings. She had enough to cover half of the fee for year one. The money for the other half and for year two, Mory did not have it; but she was confident that she would figure out when the time would come; she just had to get started. She intended to save a quarter of her income each month. This extreme saving project also meant she would squeeze everything else and keep the bare minimum to live. Even if it meant selling stuff from her house, Mory did not care, she would do it. Money was not going to be a showstopper for her MBA project.

So Mory took the first step to obtain her MBA by applying for an admission to the program. This training was very much sought after by many professionals and required a special recommendation from companies for their qualified workers or from successful and well-known business leaders.

When she applied, Mory was the IT specialist in a private TV station, but she did not want the management to know about her project as it was a personal initiative, not a company planned project. She gathered all the required documents and requested admission for the next session in autumn. The selection committee looked at the applications and published the list of the elected fifty: Mory's name was not there.

There was a profound disappointment in her heart when she found out she was not among the selected applicants. However, this did not stop Mory from continuing the started extreme saving plan. In fact, a few weeks after the list was published, she started the preparations to apply for the next year. She reflected and asked herself why she was not selected and what she could do the next time to put all chances on her side and ensure selection.

Mory asked the question to everyone who knew anything about the executive MBA program. Some of the information she collected from her search was:

- Applicants sent by companies having a great reputation, leaders in their industry field were among the first to be selected.
- Applicants with recommendations from well-known business people were also selected.
- Applicants from the governmental institution were also privileged.

If after picking from these three top categories there were some free spots left, only then would the selection committee consider individuals not known by their birth or by the reputation of their employers.

In 2004, as soon as admission was opened for the program, Mory prepared all her documents and applied again. This time around, in order to boost her application, she worked her network of university alumni who had relations with some people closed to the selection committee. Her sister knew a university friend who previously worked as a personal assistant to the current director of the commerce school. The lady - Carla - asked Mory to prepare all her documents and send them to her so that she would bring them in person to the director with a personal recommendation for selection. Mory did all as requested by Carla. Then, again came the time for the publication of the selected fifty. This time again, the name of Mory was still nowhere to be found.

Mory called Carla to inform her she had not been selected and to ask if there was anything that could explain why she was not selected. Carla said she was very shocked as well but that she would verify and get back to Mory. After the investigation, it appeared that the director never saw the file of Mory. Carla came to see the director with the application of Mory and found he was out of the country. She left the file with the assistant with the note "Important" and it was to be handed to the director as soon as he would be back.

When the director returned, the assistant had forgotten completely about the file given by Carla...this is why the file never reached him and why Mory was not selected.

A sad coincidence, right? But one good point to all of this is the determination of Mory who continued to squeeze her expenses and maintained her saving routine. She was determined to get that training no matter what or how long it would take for her to be selected. Even the failure to be chosen in the last two years did not decrease her desire, make her back off or forget about her dream.

Looking back on the second application process, to get acceptance, Mory saw the following flaws:

1. She completely relied on Carla for the deposit of her application and her selection, instead of doing herself what was officially required, and have Carla and her network as just as an additional layer to back up her candidacy.
2. When she dropped the file at the rector assistant's office as Carla demanded, she did not follow up. Regular follow-up calls to Carla would have helped to keep her application from staying on the assistant's shelf.

In preparation for the admission class of September 2005, Mory worked on her relationships with the management of the TV station where she was working. She shared with them her desire to develop herself by taking an MBA education. She took the time to explain and show the executives how such a qualification would benefit not only herself as an individual, but the added value it would have on her involvement with the company. The TV station was planning to open a second channel in the coming months. This meant more technology, equipment, software, and people to be involved, and no doubt, it would benefit the company if Mory could go beyond the operational inputs she currently provided to take on more strategic tasks regarding the technology department.

Mory's pitch worked because the General Manager and the CEO agreed to sign not one but two separate recommendation letters. The first from the General Manager was a company recommendation. The second letter from the CEO was the personal recommendation of an internationally well known, successful businessman.

With these two recommendation letters, her application documents and immovable determination, Mory applied for the cohort of autumn 2005. She deposited the application herself at the university; she confirmed with the admission office that everything required was in her application. Mory also regularly called the office to check if the list of successful applicants was released. Her regular calls and visits to the admission office made her known to the university staff who named her the very motivated TV candidate. The day the list of selected applicants was released, she got a call from the Admissions Office to inform her that the list was published. Mory hurried to consult the list and had the joy that day to confirm that she had just graduated from being an MBA dreamer to an MBA student.

Mory had seen herself as an MBA graduate for the past three years, so the long hours of studies, research, group work, exams after nine hours at work as she was doing the programme, and at the same time carrying out all the tasks at the TV station as an IT professional were anticipated. It was tough, but Mory rather saw herself through this stretching time, the sure way to accomplish her MBA goal. She always told herself, "Just a few more months, and I will be able to modify my signature to add my MBA credentials after it…".

The two years training flew quickly, then came the graduation.

On that memorable day, family and friends were so proud and congratulated her because they had seen how determined Mory was. They knew that it took three applications in three years before Mory could be selected, but she kept saving and applying for selection They saw how she reduced her purchases to the bare minimum to finance her MBA. They were aware how stressful it had been for Mory to complete the tuition payment for year two. MBA Graduation day was a great and memorable day for Mory, her determination had paid off, and she was a confirmed, official MBA.

Just four years back, the MBA credential was just an idea that Mory had, and now she had completed the training, had graduated and was part of the MBA elite class.

A few years later, Mory had to apply the same resilience and determination to immigrate to Canada, and to date, she successfully continues to go after her dreams.

As she did, you can too!

As you keep moving towards that goal with unwavering determination to get there, wearing the characteristics of mental toughness coupled with daily actions towards the set goal, ready to adapt and to learn; discouragement and turning back are NOT considered options in your mindset, you will surely get there, reach your goal and win the prize.

No matter where you are right now in the pursuit of your current goals, keep going, do that one more action because your arrival is guaranteed.

As you continue daily to exercise towards that goal, persistently moving each step of the way, allowing nothing to take you off your track, no obstacle or dissuasion of any sort to block your way, there will be no other outcome than reaching the goal you had in mind, the receipt of that earned prize carrying the label:

The winner is... YOU!

About Judith Glory

Judith Glory Modjoc, ESSEC business school MBA, is a dynamic and passionate entrepreneur who loves to help women in their career and business, be their best version ever. As she regularly says in her workshops and seminars, *"Let's bring out all the glory in you!"*

In her early years as an entrepreneur, Judith won a prestigious award from the Mandessi Bell Foundation for young entrepreneurs in Cameroon. After her immigration to Canada in 2011, Judith followed an entrepreneurship program with McGill University. Even though still a newcomer, in 2012 Judith re-ignited her entrepreneurship dreams and once again successfully launched a Web Marketing company.

She is actively involved in helping prospective entrepreneurs and start-ups with organizations such as local Chamber of Commerce, Femmessor, Yes Montreal, and various other organizations where she volunteers as mentor or business coach.

Totally bilingual (English and French), Judith Glory is the author of an upcoming book in French – *La Fille au Cœur brisé-*, where she let the woman in her go through the ups and downs of heartbreaks. This book project aims to help women think and reflect on how they manage their relationships, what they can do or put in place so as not to be defined by their emotions or be victims of their heart. For those who made some wrong decisions, Judith shows in the book how they can learn from their mistakes and successfully fail forward.

Apart from co-authoring *The Will to Win* with Brian Tracy, Judith Glory is also working on a new book project in English, to help prospective or young entrepreneurs start out right and not disappear after a few months. This book will show exactly how to successfully launch a business that will blossom and thrive many years after the start.

Judith Glory is a leadership Expert, Coach, Teacher, Trainer and Speaker certified by John Maxwell himself. As an active John Maxwell Team member, she is fully licensed to use and train organizations with the John Maxwell curriculum and programs such as:

- Leadership Gold
- Becoming a Person of Influence
- Everyone Communicates, Few Connect
- Sometimes You Win, Sometimes You Learn
- 15 Invaluable Laws of Growth
- How to Be a REAL Success
- Put Your Dreams to the Test
- and many more ...

Judith has been involved with well-known organizations throughout the world on various continents such as Apple, IBM, a major financial institution in North America, Deutsche Welle Television, CFAO Group, IOF (International organization of La Francophonie), AFNOG (African Network Operators Group), AfricaCERT and much more.

Judith is a happy mother. As such, she knows the daily juggles of working moms to make it work with job and family demands. She also knows the hesitation women have with regards to job transition or quitting a job to start their own businesses.

Judith Glory has this huge burden in her heart to give her all, to motivate and help women tap into their huge potential, to go for their dreams and achieve their career or business goals, allowing nothing and no one to stop them, not even themselves. Her passion to bring out all the glory in each woman is simply unrelenting.

CHAPTER 11

"WIN...WHAT?"

BY JOSEPH J. KRANZ, PhD

WHERE DOES IT START?

A good friend, Phil (*not his real name*), was a successful architect and creator of a design/build firm that grew from a couple of employees to a multi-million-dollar firm in a few years constructing magnificent, high end houses. Everything they did was of the highest quality and esthetically admired by all. His wife was bubbly, intelligent and devout. Both of his children were scholars and athletes at a private preparatory school. They had beautiful houses, drove high-end cars and frequently vacationed in exotic places. Phil was friendly, but never seemed particularly happy or comfortable in his skin. When his children had athletic events, Phil attended one out of three times, almost never during the week. He and his wife socialized and hosted grand garden parties for friends and clients.

Then it all came crashing down. A severe and geographically wide-spread recession occurred. To grow and keep up with projects in his sales pipeline Phil had borrowed against his assets, including his personal property. Deals were cancelled, re-negotiated or financing became unavailable. He went bankrupt in a virtual instant. His wife decided that her calling was not mother and house-wife but to serve a greater good. One of his children became addicted to opiates and the other pregnant.

Understating Phil's feelings, he became intensely depressed. Still, he muddled through the confusing muck of bankruptcy, divorce and single parenting of sorely-distressed children.

We met one Sunday to listen to a small outdoor Jazz concert and have coffee. He needed friendship and a compassionate ear.

"You know, Joe, I thought I was on top of the world. I was winning. My company had lots of work; I was creating and building great designs. Money was 'rolling in'. I thought I had a soulmate for life and my kids were OK. I can't believe my life collapsed so easily."

I said, *"You know Phil, you're a talented and soulful person, but you've always seemed to me to be just a bit unhappy."*

"You're insightful and right." he said. *"I feel like I was doing everything well, had great goals and plans and I was proud of myself, but I always had a gut feeling that I wasn't trying to win playing the right game...and even now I don't know what the game should be!"*

Then I knew that I could be of real value to help Phil recover his life and find "the" game for him and enable him to create a best life for himself.

Many people believe that loved ones and living environment are the keys to our happiness. They are, in fact, externalities. There is no question that they are important to our human condition, but they will not make us happy. Being THERE is an "inside job".

Some people feel that there is no way to proceed. Many people who are driven to win at the externalities of life feel that to achieve inner happiness one cannot take specific steps, that there is some sort of magic that must just happen. In many spiritual traditions, such as Buddhism, adherents are taught to seek a psychic place of peace and completeness. The facts are that the adherents already own that place, it is just that they don't have the address. That place, that IT, is more like a motor home than a fixed residence.

A well-known book by Sheldon Kopp, *"If you meet the Buddha on the road, kill him (1976)"*, posits that one must accept the fact that one cannot find the place because there is no such place, and that the journey or path is what one must accept as the IT. That is only partially true. The place moves with a person because the place is not a separate place at all… it resides within oneself as opposed to you trying to reside in it. Looking outside for IT is fruitless. Since it moves with you there is no way to get there; you are already there but don't know it. IT is you, inseparable from the universe.

So, the problem is, how does one go about becoming aware and appreciating this place? Is there a way to enhance it? A humble wise man, Sydney Banks, came to an insight about the structure of our inner and outer interface with the universe which shows that we have what we need to live the life we want. Other "self-help" gurus, such as the renowned and respected Steven Covey offered spiritual and principle-based methods for achieving a success or "winning". There is a prolific library of self-help gurus, books and tapes. My insight is that looking for guidance from outside is backward thinking. The guidance one seeks is already available inside. Learned Yogic gurus will tell you that they cannot show you the path or the portal to happiness and peace … winning at life. They, and all the self-help books, are powerless to show you the way. You can only be helped to understand how you think and how you create your own reality. And IT is your own reality. No one else has it.

So why am I writing this paper? I believe that there are some clues to finding the way to finding the way in the assembled wisdom of all these other seekers and insightful thinkers. I also believe that there is a process, a "meta-process" so to speak (which is why I repeated *"finding the way"* above), which one can follow to find the way to find the way. Not so humbly, I have titled this meta-process: "Create a Best Life". Seeking winning at life, however YOU define it, is a creative act. And the way you go about it exemplifies your innate creativity. You are in the game of creating your life with your objectives... your true self in mind. But beware, you cannot push your way through this; you must understand first who is truly YOU, including the context and the feelings that go with it.

PROCESS SKELETON

Consider doing questioning that will lead you to answers in five areas:

1. Find meaning in being – find what you truly want... phrase the question and keep asking until it goes deep... the answer will come and don't be frightened by it if it seems outrageous, it's not, it's "in-rageous"... from inside you.
2. Identify principles – describe the core principles you use in life ... consciously and intuitively... ask the questions.
3. Define purpose in the sphere of influence – no one can address all purposes in the universe... identify the soft edges of what you feel is where you want to operate.
4. Create the mission path – for those of you who are drivers and struggling pushers of activity, this is yours... define your mission and how you think you want to get there.
5. Do, check/evaluate, reflect... remember the famous words of Yoda from the *Star Wars* stories: *"Do. Or do not. There is no try."*... go all the way; if you've done the work above this you are in a safe place that you can do (there may be bumps but that is the universe... you are not what life gives you... you have the ability to live it to the fullest and best).

HOW DO YOU DO IT?

You don't! Years ago, I started to study Naturalistic Decision-Making. Curiously, what I found was that we humans do not make analytic, coldly-logical decisions. We make decisions based on our emotions, clearly described by Antonio Damasio in *"Descartes' Error: Emotion, Reason, and the Human Brain (1994)"*. And we cannot get directly to our center of emotions via just our brain and our cognitive awareness; it is a physiological impossibility. To paraphrase Alan Jasanoff, director of the MIT Center for Neurobiological Engineering, in *The Biological Mind (2018)*, 'the activation of emotions is distributed throughout our body.' In other words, the whole decision process is a holistic mechanism in our being. So, what? To make it even more bewildering, we make a decision before we are aware that we have done so. *(ibid.)*

Given that this situation is true, how does one make ANY reasonable decisions about their path in life? Again, don't even try, because *"…there is no."* In fact, "trying" is the worst approach because it will only lead to frustration and misdirection… and don't believe some self-help gurus on this, goal setting is frequently based on contaminated thinking. A person can set reasonable goals based on what they know. The problem is with what they don't know and can't get to directly. Your foundational thinking, and latent, unseen assumptions can trip one up and these bases for decision-making reveal themselves later in stress, dissatisfaction and disappointment.

So, what is the good news? Hopefully it is obvious that I wouldn't be painting this inscrutable paradox to create despair. There are answers and, again, the answers are not answers, they are questions. We are led to intuitive answers through questioning. No matter how hard you try, you cannot make an emotionless decision. It is because your center of valuing everything is seated in your body and its complex interactions. So, when you ask questions and are persistent at it, the answers form. I used to have a byline of "The right answers are in the right questions." I have found through experience that this is always true and there is recent research which confirms it. (Hal Gregersen, *Better Brainstorming: Focus on questions, not answers, for breakthrough insights.,* Harvard Business Review, March-April 2018.)

Earlier in this paper, I listed 5 objectives. These are critical objectives to achieve your best life. BUT, you cannot successfully approach them directly. You must go through a process of questioning. There are several well-established questioning methods: Taiichi Ohno's five times questions, Voice of the Customer (VOC) questioning, "Beautiful Questions" and others. One of my favorites is based in journalistic questioning as codified brilliantly by Rudyard Kipling in one of his poems:

> *I keep six honest serving men*
> *(They taught me all I knew);*
> *Their names are What and Why and When*
> *And How and Where and Who.*

Each one of these methods, and others, will work. The key is to continue to ask questions of the questions. Be utterly persistent and go into depth; your deepest thoughts and emotions will be revealed. It has been reported that Albert Einstein once said: *"If I had an hour to solve a problem and my life depended on the solution, I would spend the first 55 minutes determining the proper question to ask ... for once I know the proper question, I could solve the problem in less than five minutes."* Einstein spent over 90% of his time and effort in asking questions. When you ask your questions, DO NOT try to answer them. Keep asking and go deeper. Do not even think about solutions; they will contaminate your questioning process and lead you to paths only of apparent possibilities... none of which may be the answer. Your intuition will show you the answer or the approach to the ultimate answer if you don't get in the way by jumping to solutions. What may seem an impossible or impracticable problem will reveal its solution when you have questioned enough.

YOUR best life depends on asking questions. The answers will become evident. Only then can you create your best life. So, whether you are trying to find your life's meaning or mission or path, keep asking questions. The answers will come, and you will WIN at life.

By the way, Phil found his best life and is a truly happy person. Once he had questioned and questioned with my careful guidance, he came to the realization that he is at core, an artist. His creative architectural focus fulfills him, but his commercial efforts fail him. He is now a lead artist, designer and architect for dramatic and beautiful resort communities constructed by others and has recovered financially. His wife is happily in a convent living her true self and they have a peaceful and spiritual relationship. He has been able to guide his children to begin fulfilling their lives with serenity and purpose.

References:

–Damasio, Antonio (1994). *Descartes' Error: Emotion, Reason, and the Human Brain.* New York: G.P. Putnam.
–Gregerson, Hal. (March-April 2018). *Better Brainstorming.* Harvard Business Review, Pages 64-71.
–Jasanoff, Alan. (2018). *The Biological Mind.* New York: Basic Books.
–Kopp, Sheldon B. (1976). *If You Meet the Buddha on the Road, Kill Him!* Palo Alto, California: Science and Behavior Books, Inc.

About Joseph

Joseph J. Kranz, PhD guides his clients and compeers on life's journeys to create a best life for themselves. His corporate, non-profit, government and other institutional clients benefit from his elegant, efficient and economical processes to optimize operations, enhance abilities and clarify insights to achieve genuine alignment with purpose, objectives and methods.

With life-long experiences and education in naturalistic decision-making, his background has led to an understanding and employment of practices which realistically help others to discover and elucidate their own core principles. Once there, they are guided to enable themselves to follow paths which optimize their experiences and realization of their vision.

Dr. Kranz has, and continues to aid, individuals and organizations internationally; he has worked in many countries (e.g., Afghanistan, Bulgaria, Colombia, Egypt, Estonia, Philippines, Poland, etc.) and contexts. While his individual client list is confidential, it currently includes people in a variety of careers: trial attorney; motivational speaker; Guinness Book of World Records athlete and trainer; medical professional; singer; recording and performance guitarist; human resources professional; chef; house painter; electrician; film music composer and producer. Successful engagements with international organizations and programs included governments, manufacturers, and institutions in: high technology, ocean sciences, National Oceanic and Atmospheric Administration (NOAA), basic science, charitable human services, education, emergency medicine, police and military, sales and marketing, US Peace Corps, US Agency for International Development (USAID), politics and environmental and primate protection advocacy. He also has spoken at conferences on many topics.

A widower, Dr. Kranz lives in California and has two adult children. He is a restorer and collector of classic cars, a water color artist, organic gardener and poet. He is available to assist a limited number of clients who will be mutually qualified for engagement. He smiles a lot.

Contact him at:

- info@createabestlife.com

CHAPTER 12

WINNERS SHOW UP

BY JIM SHUTE

THE GOLDEN HOUR

We called it "the golden hour." The year was 1982. The technology of choice for me and my fellow Account Executives— trying to connect with prospects in Fortune 500 companies— was a telephone, supported by a rudimentary CRM system (a set of 3 X 5 index cards with prospect names/phone numbers). Between 9 and 10 AM—the golden hour—was the best window of opportunity to catch executive decision-makers while they were still sitting at their desk sipping their first cup of coffee and reading the Wall Street Journal, ahead of their first scheduled meeting at 10 o'clock.

If you caught them unaware, an executive might pick up the phone themselves, but usually your call was screened by their secretary. That is, if you had access to the direct-dial phone number for your prospect (if not, there was pre-screening by the operator at the company switchboard). Of course, getting the name of the right person to call in the first place involved a trip to the library to search the Advertiser's Red Book (a reference guide about the size of two Manhattan phone books), listing Fortune 500 companies and their executives/titles. Business protocol dictated mailing (yep, via US Postal Service) a single-page typed business letter of introduction a week or so prior to reaching out by phone. The process was arduous compared with looking up somebody on LinkedIn and shooting them a message.

DIGITAL MAKES IT EASIER...AND HARDER

Despite the digital resources at our disposal today—enabling "virtual relationship building" on a mass basis—there is no substitute for one-on-one, in-person interaction with prospects. This is especially true with professional services, complex sales, and big-ticket items.

But getting appointments in the first place, and then moving those contacts into and through the sales funnel, is harder than ever. That same digital technology that makes it easier to connect also makes getting a prospect's attention and time to sit down for an introductory/exploratory meeting even more difficult.

If relationships matter so much, what's the best way to get an initial meeting with a prospective client? Once face-to-face, how do you transition from a "nice conversation" into something more productive? And if that initial meeting is successful enough to warrant follow-up, how do you do so in a way that is value-adding, intelligent, and moves the relationship forward?

It requires "showing up" in these three phases:

- Showing up in the first place: getting meetings with prospects (sounds simple, isn't easy).
- Showing up in initial meetings: making an impression, determining "fit," and selling the next meeting (or extricating yourself as fast and respectfully as you can).
- Showing up in your follow-up activities to move the process forward: "intelligent follow-up" to build productive relationships (*not* "just checkin' in").

In selling over $50 million in professional services during my career, I've learned effective ways to get, make, and follow up on over 10,000 face-to-face sales calls. This chapter will help you to build or expand your portfolio of professional relationships that produce results for your business—focusing on the initial phase: *Showing Up in the First Place.*

WHAT IS IT THAT YOU'RE SELLING?

When my company builds training programs for our clients, we divide the learning into three areas: mindsets, skill sets, and tool sets. *Mindset* is the starting point because it guides how any skills or tools get applied.

Many sales professionals fail (or make things more difficult than they should be) in their attempts to set meetings with prospects because they think they need to sell their product or service at this stage. A more enlightened approach might be to view it as "selling yourself," but it's even simpler than that. At this early phase of the sales process, the only thing you can possibly sell— and should think about selling—is an *appointment.*

Over the years, two "laws of physics" have emerged that guide my thinking—my mindset—around appointment setting:

1. Nobody buys anything, ever, during the first visit (at least not for big-ticket, complex products or services). So, don't bother trying to sell anything other than an appointment at this stage.
2. Nobody makes a purchase decision alone. Decisions (at least any major ones) require consultation and collaboration by multiple people in an organization. One of the goals of an initial meeting with anyone should be to meet others involved in the decision process (selling more *appointments*).

With your mind set on just selling *meetings* at this phase, the goal is focused and attainable. You can then start applying the *skills* of appointment-setting.

FIND A STARTING POINT

Many businesses have marketing efforts that generate prospects. Others might require you to identify prospects through your own resourcefulness. In the digital age, it's tough for anyone to hide, so *identifying* prospects isn't the problem. At some point *outreach* is required to get a meeting with someone who can influence the purchase of your product... and that's where the challenge begins.

When requesting an initial meeting, it's always best to start with some sort of connection, however slim.

- Start with somebody you know in an organization and work your way up, down, or across, to somebody who has an interest or need for your product/service.
- Find a colleague in your network to make an introduction, using connections from your current client list, your alma mater, or even your recreational/social networks (LinkedIn is great for this).
- If you've worked for similar organizations or in a similar industry, mention that, as your connection (it's thin, but people love to know what's going on with the competition or in the industry).

No connection? Start your outreach at the top of the organization and get "referred down" to someone accordingly.

- Seek guidance and direction using phrases like, "I was hoping you might be able to help me," or "perhaps you can direct me to the appropriate person."
- Once referred, you can plausibly state to a prospect, "Sandy Johnston's office suggested I contact you...," as your connection.

CHOOSE THE BEST "MEDIA"

The modern world offers many options for making initial contact with a prospect. I've found that most prospects prefer some sort of information "in hand" before agreeing to a meeting. This establishes an initial connection. It involves sending a brief, compelling message describing who you are and why a prospect would benefit from meeting with you.

Here are a few possibilities:

Email: Still a standard, accepted method when reaching out to folks in corporations or organizations. Its challenges include getting an email address in the first place (use your "connection" if possible), getting your mail through spam filters, and then getting it opened and reviewed by the prospect (amidst the scores of other emails jamming their inbox).

Text: If you have a prospect's mobile number, you've likely established some sort of connection already. While challenging to craft a sufficiently compelling message using text, it can be useful in follow-up to a previous conversation or as quick correspondence to request an appointment.

Messaging: (e.g., LinkedIn messaging.) A variation on email, with the "connection" presumably pre-established via your LinkedIn connection.

Phone: Direct and synchronous, a phone call cuts straight to the chase. It can be challenging to get a prospect's phone number (direct office line or mobile). And with caller ID, getting someone to pick up an unknown number is rare. Consider likely times when a prospect might answer (before 10 AM when meetings start, or after 4:30 when the day is winding down) and be prepared with your messaging.

In-Person: (e.g., at Networking events.) This is an excellent way to meet prospects and attempt to set a follow-up appointment on the spot. Or use these speed-dating meetings to establish your "connection" for later follow-up ("we were introduced briefly at the ACE conference…").

Snail-Mail (with phone follow-up). While old/slow technology, a well-written, personally signed letter (with the right messaging) can project professionalism. Use the letter as your connection when following up by phone to request an appointment.

Choose media based on your circumstances/preferences. Bottom line: the approach (selling an appointment) and messaging (see below) are the same regardless of media.

CRAFT YOUR MESSAGE

Whether you're making initial contact digitally, via phone, or in person, there are some guidelines that will help dramatically increase your success rate:

1. **Keep it brief**. Five or six sentences, with two or three bullet points, max, is about all that busy people can take, regardless of media.

2. **The Subject line matters**. Succinct and straightforward works best. If you're selling an appointment, allude to that in the subject line. Hyperbole often lands your message in the spam folder, or on deaf ears.

3. **Lead with your connection.** This should ideally answer the question, "Why should I continue reading/listening?" The answer (from the prospect's perspective) should be: respecting the colleague who referred them, or access to useful information.

4. **Get to your purpose quickly.** You want to schedule a brief, exploratory meeting to learn about the prospect's plans/priorities and to share information about you/your company.

5. **Suggest that there is value in meeting with you.** The possibility of gaining information and insight can be quite compelling to a prospect.
   - "We've done some unique things in your industry…"
   - "Your counterparts at [related companies] have found that…"
   - "I'd like to share an idea or two that might have application for you…"

Give them a thirst (not a drink), by *alluding* to the value that you will share when you meet. If you claim to have an idea to share, make sure you have one to share by the time you meet!

6. **Make it non-threatening.** These sorts of phrases help to keep it pressure-less:
   - You are seeking a brief "exploratory meeting…"
   - "20–30 minutes at your convenience…"
   - …to "learn about your interests/needs/plans/priorities." (People respect folks who want to learn something… especially when it's learning about *them*.)
   - …to "see if makes sense to talk further" or "if there is a 'fit'."

Worst case (the prospect is thinking), they invest 30 minutes of their time and receive an idea or insight, with no strings attached.

7. **Make it easy to say "yes."** Provide all the information needed for prospects to accept your offer:
   - Provide alternative meeting dates and time windows.
   - Mention that you are going to be in their area/building anyway. This relieves any "guilt" the prospect may feel about potentially wasting your time.

Even if I don't yet have an appointment in a prospect's area/ building at the time I request a meeting, I have no qualms including this phrase because if they accept, I will indeed be there after all…and can then use this "anchor" appointment to piggy-back other meetings around it, using the same technique.

8. **Project a confident professional demeanor.** We talked earlier about mindset. Your message (written or spoken) needs to project that you *have value to add, and the right to meet with the prospect to share it.* Back when there were secretaries my calls were screened by "What is the purpose of your call?" After floundering around with vague responses (and getting unceremoniously "screened"), I finally tried, "I'm calling to schedule an appointment," stated with confidence, like I had every right to do so. My success rate at speaking with their boss, and setting appointments, increased dramatically.

Finally, keep the focus on the prospect. A good test is to print out your message and circle every "you" (referring the prospect) and every "I" or "we." The "you's" should outnumber the "I's" in a prospect-centered message.

"OUT-REASONABLE THEM"

One of my early bosses used to say that to schedule appointments, you need to "out-reasonable" the prospect. Effectively, present your appointment proposition in such a way that it would be unreasonable to say no.

Think about it from the prospect's perspective. Would it be reasonable to meet with somebody who:

- Has a connection to your industry, company, or someone you know?
- Has alluded to providing some sort of useful insights or information during the meeting?
- Has suggested mutual exploration, to see if there is a fit?
- Is only requesting 30 minutes?
- Is going to be in your area/building anyway?

Using these guidelines—and tailoring them to your product/ service and your personal style—will dramatically improve the odds of your prospects saying "sure, why don't you come by for 30 minutes next Thursday afternoon."

FOLLOW UP AS NEEDED

Just last week I finally sat down to meet with a prospect I had been chasing for over 3 years and 25 emails. In Email #25, I wrote:

As I reviewed the email thread below, I realized that it has been over three years since you took on your new position, and we've been trying to schedule a get-together. Pro-Active has certainly grown and evolved during that time, and worked on some interesting projects in your area of responsibility. If you think you might have interest/needs for our types of services, would it make sense to schedule a web-conference to review/discuss? At the current rate we might end up meeting sometime in 2020, and I want to get out in front of that! ☺(Yep, smiley-face included.)

The meeting that ensued was well worth the effort, the wait, and the persistence required (it created two active proposal opportunities).

As part of your "campaign of reasonableness," it is appropriate to follow up; and if you feel a particular prospect is worth it, to persist until they tell you to stop, or until you've secured an initial meeting. Here are some guidelines that I follow:

- Give prospects one week to respond. After that, it's fair game for you to follow up. If following up on an email:
  - Keep it brief, referencing your original correspondence, and using the same guidelines to "out-reasonable" the prospect—only briefer!
  - Suggest that you are "following up," "circling back," or "checking to ensure my earlier note didn't slip through the cracks."

- Enlist the help of an administrative assistant, colleague, or networking contact.
  - Determine the prospect's direct-dial or mobile number, and a convenient time to reach out—as appropriate.
- Follow up with a phone call or text message.

Repeat the process as many times as required to reach closure (an appointment, or a request to cease-and-desist), or for as long as you feel a prospect warrants.

KEEP AT IT

The more you work at crafting your connections and reaching out to prospects (and the more you try!) the better your "hit rate" will get at securing appointments. However, this is still sales— and like baseball, becoming a .300 hitter is about as good as it ever gets. Even with my skill, experience, and long-established professional networks, I'm doing well if one-in-three of my outreach attempts (typically via email) get a response on the first try.

Keep these guidelines in mind...

- Cultivate connections
- Sell appointments (not products/services)
- Craft a concise introductory message
- Make it unreasonable not to meet
- Follow up appropriately and persistently
  ...and keep at it!

As you refine your approach, you will "show up" more often— and build a more productive business network in the process.

About Jim

Jim Shute has been helping people to succeed through learning and professional development for over 35 years. A career-long sales professional, Jim is founder and president of Pro-Active Learning, Inc., a company that develops and delivers sales and customer service training programs for companies in premium market sectors. Along the way he has sold over $50 million in professional services and made over 10,000 face-to-face sales calls. More importantly he has been able to establish, build, and maintain productive client relationships through his practical and personal sales and communication approaches. Jim and his company have designed and conducted sales training programs to help clients and their employees do the same.

A graduate of The Pennsylvania State University, Jim began his career in the corporate communications field, selling and producing corporate presentations, meetings, and video programs for Fortune 500 companies. In the early 1990's, he became involved in the corporate training arena, working for Philadelphia and Princeton-based consulting firms before becoming a partner in a corporate training, systems, and incentive/recognition provider.

Jim has both developed and overseen development of instructional programs in a wide variety of media including seminars/workshops, self-study programs, interactive multimedia, eLearning, and special events. Clients have included Bristol-Myers, Correct Craft and Johnson & Johnson—along with a 'who's who' among premium automotive brands (Audi, Aston-Martin, BMW, Jaguar, Land Rover, Lexus, and Porsche).

In 2001, Jim formed Pro-Active Learning to implement solutions that deliver not just information, but improved capability to people—converting "programs from headquarters into practices in the field or at retail." He has extensive skills and experience in the areas of analysis, design, and development of content/information, and delivery of the resulting knowledge and skills to people within organizations. Pro-Active Learning has developed and delivered sales, customer experience, and process improvement initiatives that have produced measurable and sustained results for its clients—including a Brandon Hall Excellence Award for a 500%+ improvement in sales-lead follow-up activities.

It was the late 1980's, when Jim first became an avid student of Brian Tracy and Jim Cathcart, listening to their audio cassette series while driving the NJ Turnpike en route to sales calls. He learned to apply that knowledge effectively—and it is from that successful application that many of the methods in this chapter were developed.

You can connect with Jim at:

- Email: jshute@pro-activelearning.com
- Twitter: www.twitter.com/JimShute
- Facebook: www.facebook.com/proactiveperformance.doylestown.pa

CHAPTER 13

TRIANGLE SUCCESS: MASTERING FEAR, HAPPINESS, AND MOTIVATION TO WIN

BY DR. THANI ALMHEIRI

Thinking of transforming yourself from employee to self-employed is an idea that a lot of people have. However, people rarely see that this act is actually a very brave one, one of transforming your dreams into reality.

One day in 2014, a chance meeting with friends had me considering doing just that. I spent the day in Dubai for a conference and met with some friends for coffee. While there we discussed what to do with our futures at the next stage of our lives. Establishing a new business was at the top of all of our lists, and for me, I'd been thinking about building a company where I could do some importing and provide myself with a steady and reliable income. It's always enticing to talk things through with people you trust, and this time they disagreed with each other. One friend was encouraging, while warning that the importing business was very competitive. The other friend was warier, saying that the business would need too much work and capital to start up. The talk was very tentative, because my friend had fears about losing money, but I knew that thinking about the success was the key. From my perspective, one should think about success rather than the monetary value of an idea, as the monetary success will always come second.

When our meeting was over, I drove home thinking about all that had transpired and my desire to mould my future into something successful. My friends were stuck thinking about the dangers of establishing a new business and were focused on potential loss rather than potential success. Of course, its excellent to consult others, but you must also listen to your inner voice, and mine was telling me, 'Go start your business and don't waste any more time just talking about it. You are already a talented business person. Just do it!'

I explored this inner voice then and I've learned that its really about three key things. If you pay keen attention to these things you are bound to align yourself with the kind of success you've been dreaming of!

A. **First: You must physically be in a quiet, calm place** to hear and feel what your inner voice is telling you. If you only spend time in noisy and crowded places you won't be able to connect with what drives you.

B. **Second: Tap into the images in your mind** that come up when you think about the business idea that you have. Do they have certain themes or energy? Do certain things appear repeatedly when you think about what your business might achieve? These images are the guiding force which will help you to change your life. For example, before going to sleep, one might see an image of a car or a book title or a sign of something related to your business idea.

C. **Third: Most importantly, understand the types of feelings you have** when it comes to the business you are picturing. The most common of these feelings are **fear, happiness and motivation**. Understanding the way these work within yourself, and how to use them to your advantage, is key to winning!

1. <u>Fear</u>

If you lead your life with fear, you cannot win. You might fear losing money or the burden of a busy life. You might fear moving outside your comfort zone. These fears are your enemies and can cause you to give up your business idea. If you start a great idea with fear attached to it, it will be a great idea but in the wrong time and place rather than a great idea in the right place and time! Fear is a fog that prevents you from seeing your idea in real life. So, drop off fear from your life if you want to win!

2. <u>Happiness</u>

Second, the feeling of happiness is very important. Sometimes, if you are overly happy, then you might mislead yourself to be in a virtual reality type of business. You will oversee some important realistic indicators that you need to assess during the business planning practice. An example is being happy to open a fast food restaurant does not assure you sales if the location has no verifiable customer counts. So, don't forget that to do due diligence on the idea and check all the important success factors.

3. <u>Motivation</u>

Third, feeling motivated about the idea that you have. Motivation is a key factor to your future success, so it's imperative that you clearly differentiate between motivation and feeling happy. Feeling happy about an idea you invented is not like feeling motivated to implement the idea. Happiness is associated with abstraction while motivation is associated with energy and implementation. Happiness describes nice and great ideas, while motivation describes realistic and practical ideas. Happiness is an external characteristic of your feelings of self-satisfaction and glory, while motivation is an internal characteristic allowing you to take action, secure resources, and do the things you want to do to start your business.

Fear, happiness, and motivation—or as I call them, **FHM**—are factors of great ideas will to win.

I went from thinking to action just in one day after that meeting with my friends, because I was very motivated to start my business idea – establishing a retail importing company. I checked my FHM factors, clearly identified my inner voice call and secured my motivation to start a winning business! The next step was to identify three key features or quality characteristics of the products I wanted to sell:

1) The first one was uniqueness of the products - products must be unknown to the customers and have different shapes or forms.
2) The second feature is quality of products contents/ ingredients.
3) The third feature was good and competitive.

Equipped with those product features and my FHM factors, I started searching for products to distribute. I was amazed by the products I could bring, and the challenge was which would be the product that would meet customers' needs and satisfy their desire to buy. After three months of online research, I got nothing attractive. I was looking for the product that would make me say "Yes!" or "Wow!" but still I could not find it.

Eventually, I came across products that caught my attention. I did my homework by searching and reading about the products and the manufacturer. This manufacturer produced very good products that were sold in more than twenty-five countries. Then, I contacted the manufacturer and submitted my business proposal to be their distributor. After negotiations for almost three months, I was granted the exclusive rights to distribute these products. I decided to start with twelve different types of products. I was very happy, so I decided to rent a small office, hired two people, and contracted with a logistics company to handle the export and import affairs and product storage. I ordered the first shipment of products and contracted eleven retail hypermarkets to sell the products. The challenge was a very logistics-intensive business with expenses such as shelf-renting fees, product registration fees, customs fees, etc. I fully invested until I sold all of the first shipment of 5,000 items. Things were going well! So, I ordered the second shipment, which was 10,000 items.

Then, another challenge arose. While I was in the middle of selling this order, I got an email from the manufacturer informing me that they decided to change the products' shape and costs as well as stopping the production of some other products (which were my most popular). I was shocked in that I had just barely started to gain my business profits and now was back to the drawing board. But, I would not be deterred!

I started to look and search for new products and came across mineral water from a country in South America that would be new and unique in its qualities to the market. I contacted the manufacturer, got a positive reply and drafted a contract for the product. It was a mouth-watering deal, and I signed the contract and placed the first order. A few days later, I received an invoice with bank transfer instructions. However, there was another snag when I noticed that the bank transfer instructions asked me to transfer the funds to a bank account in Europe instead of South America. So, I emailed them asking for clarification and they said, "We do not have a bank account in South America as we used a European bank account." Then, I checked with my bank and they told me it was a scam. That was a tough time again for me, but I remained positive and remembered my FHM as I moved to find another product. This time, the company was very cooperative and helpful, and it only took me a few weeks to order and receive the first batch of products. I sold the entire order within three months. This product was very healthy and of high quality. The next step was to find more like it!

During this time, it was a coincidence that I went to the same exhibition of cosmetic manufacturers where I had first talked with my friends about the business which was now successful and growing. I met a manufacturer who was selling products that I really liked. The owner was wonderful in explaining his products, and we developed a rapport which meant that I was soon invited and accepted, an invitation to visit his factory. While there, I went through the production process of the products from A to Z. I learned a lot from the process and I asked him if I could create my own brand using his factory. I started my brand which included 16 different products. I selected and designed the products with his company's help. I even invented a new product called hand wash and lotion, where you have a two-in-one hand wash and hand lotion mixed together. Then, I placed the first order for my brand, which was about 10,000 units of the sixteen product categories. I became a brand owner now, not just a distributor for another company's products. This new challenge taught me how to welcome risks and challenges and turn them into a 'will to win' spirit.

My company today in 2018 is doing well. We have thirty product categories that are sold online on top world online shopping sites. Through all these challenges, it was very helpful for me to remember that I was working toward my goal of being self-employed and successful. My 'will to win' was working for me. All of these experiences helped me to learn and become successful in my business and each challenge is a lesson for the future. The things I've learned can all be traced back to my FHM and the resulting lessons from getting out there and doing it.

Reflecting on my challenges and successes led me to think about some things to keep in mind as you start your journey to success. Think about the following four 'will to win' factors:

1. **Ideas that emerge from motivation** are different than ideas that emerge from feeling happy. The key difference is that motivational ideas guide you to take actions with all your senses, while happy ideas just make you feel happy and you dream about your business idea for a short term. However, as soon as you are challenged it is easy to give up and never take practical action.

2. **Make a motivational plan and focus on that**. Business planning is not important to start your business, but rather, motivational planning is what matters most. Motivational planning is about taking action and building your business from an operational learning perspective (learning by doing). Business planning is good but can demotivate you from your ideas. If you read any successful entrepreneur's biography, you'll discover none of them mentioned writing a business plan.

3. **Business due diligence (BDD)** is a good exercise to do by visiting and seeing similar business ideas in operation. Take the time to learn and understand similar business operations in real life by seeing, physically visiting, and meeting entrepreneurs in their business places. Ask the deepest questions about challenges first and successes later. Then spend focused time thinking about each challenge that might prevent you from starting your business.

4. **Correlate your time and actions**. Each action you are going to take must be followed by the next action within three working days. If you send an email to another business today, then after two days, if no reply is received, follow-up! Actions need to flow one after the other. If it takes you a long time to get to the next action, then your business will

be slow, and your investment will take a longer time to make good returns.

If you remember the things I've talked about here and reflect on them frequently you will have the 'will to win', and you will succeed.

About Dr. Thani

Dr. Thani Almheiri helps customers around the world get high quality products with excellent prices. He invented the FHM (Fear, Happiness, Motivation) factors for assuring a wining business action plan. Dr. Thani is one of the next century thinkers-type and leader in the retail business industry, as he developed three winning companies from scratch. He started his first company in 2004, which was a leading engineering consultancy and architectural services business.

In 2014, he established his second company in the food retail industry and was very successful in introducing a different concept of franchising in the UAE, which was based on an individual or partnership model that allowed the investor to be independent but operate within a franchise agreement. This concept allowed many entrepreneurs to expand and get their business units to grow. Then in 2015, he established a third company in retail products distribution. This company's mission is to provide customers with high quality products with excellent prices. It's about the value of products more than the value of price. Dr. Thani's background ranges from education management to entrepreneur leadership skills utilizing positive energy and forward-thinking skills. The key fundamental factors of successful retail businesses are the quality of products, uniqueness of products, and price competitiveness. This is Dr. Thani's formula for a successful retail company.

Dr. Thani is a social influencer in Twitter, as his account is a place for interaction on positive thinking, business ideas, service improvement, and 'will to win' factors and spirit. He interacts with more than 30,000 followers with perfect tweets using images and key words. He invented the term "techknolowgy" as a symbol that uses technology and knowledge to improve retail industry. He believes in pragmatic thinking in doing things in life. Dr. Thani is an Ohio State University graduate with a Ph.D. in Human and Community resources development. He has delivered many conferences papers and speeches throughout his career in education as well as at business and industry conferences. His contribution to the world of education and the retail industry is outstanding and promising.

You can contact Dr. Thani Almheiri at:

- Twitter: @techknolowgy
- Email: dr.thani@gmail.com
- LinkedIn (link):
  https://www.linkedin.com/in/thani-al-mheiri-ph-d-51861a151

CHAPTER 14

ACHIEVING ULTIMATE SUCCESS IN PERSUASION: STORYSELLING IS BELIEVING

BY JW DICKS & NICK NANTON

So, in January of 1967, Paul McCartney, then-member of the Beatles (we assume you've heard of them), was in a car accident in London. A brief rumor gripped England that Sir Paul was actually killed in the crash. The next month, the official Beatles "fanzine" verified that McCartney was, in fact, alive and well, and life went on as normal - for a while, anyway.

A little over two years later, however, in the autumn of 1969, the stress of superstardom had pulled apart the world's most popular rock group. The Beatles were splitting up, and Paul was spending more and more time in Scotland with his new wife Linda, out of the public eye.

And that's when the weirdness really kicked in. With Paul in hiding for the first time since he and his mates became superstars, the student newspaper at Drake University in Iowa printed a story that seriously asked the question, "Is Beatle Paul

McCartney Dead?" The rumor had grown in strength on the campus – and suddenly the students were hunting down clues that had supposedly been placed on the group's most recent albums. For instance, when part of the "Revolution #9" track on *The White Album* was played backwards, a voice said, "Turn me on, dead man." Others swore that, as the end of "Strawberry Fields Forever" faded away, another voice clearly said, "I buried Paul."[1]

Suddenly, Derek Taylor, the Beatles' press rep back in London, was inundated by calls – was Paul in fact deceased? He denied that he was. Because…well, he wasn't.

But then, the rumor made its way to Detroit – where another college newspaper made fun of the gossip by writing a satirical article detailing the "clues" that proved that McCartney was no longer living. Unfortunately, the story was picked up as *fact* by newspapers across the U.S. – and soon the subject was burning up the radio airwaves in New York City, among other major cities.

The "real story" was revealed as this: McCartney had died in that London car crash a few years ago. The Beatles, desperate to continue their success, had replaced him with a guy named William Campbell, the winner of a Paul McCartney look-alike contest, who coincidentally enough, *evidently sounded just like him and had the same incredible musical talent.* Huh.

Three songs were written and released by other rockers about the "death" of Paul. A television special was produced and syndicated nationally, in which a courtroom "trial" was held to decide if Paul was, in fact, dead; F. Lee Bailey, a leading celebrity lawyer at the time, cross-examined "witnesses." The verdict? Well, that was left in the hands of the viewers.

And finally, Paul McCartney decided to rise from the dead - and

---

1. John Lennon later revealed, the voice was saying "Cranberry sauce."

give an interview to *Life* magazine declaring he was alive and well – and just enjoying being "not famous" for the first time in many years.

Now, we will grant you, there have been plenty of movies about look-alikes taking over for famous people (starting with about eighty versions of *Prisoner of Zenda* over the years). But, as far as we know, there's never been an example of this actually happening in real life – let alone it happening with a worldwide superstar subject to intense media scrutiny who continued to publicly perform and create new music.

So...how could anyone swallow this story???

How could anyone believe that someone could quickly and easily take the place of someone as talented and singular as Paul McCartney was at the time? Even while new records featuring his instantly recognizable voice were still being made and released? How could anyone for a minute not only buy this whopper – but continue to spread it all across the globe?

Well, there is a very good reason many people actually believed it (or, at the very least, took it seriously) – and that's because it was *a great story*. And, as we'll see in this chapter, a great story causes people to believe fiction over fact – *because the human brain can't tell the difference.*

Scary? A little bit.

In this excerpt from our book, *StorySelling*, we'll explain exactly why this happens – and what it means in terms of what we call "StorySelling" – the process in which you tell a powerful story to create a powerful Celebrity Brand.

FACT VERSUS FICTION:
WHEN THE TRUTH DOESN'T MATTER

There are two important points we want to make about stories, points that have been backed up by tons of scientific research (which we'll discuss in detail in our book). Point one: Stories aren't necessarily a *creative* process – your brain generates and uses them as a *tool* to explain your life and what's happening around you. Point two: Good stories hit your brain in its "reward centers" – they actually cause chemical reactions that make you feel good in fundamental ways.

Now, let's apply those two points to the Paul is dead story and why it developed such a massive following, even though it was patently absurd.

To the first point, the "Paul is dead" story *explained* why Beatles fans were suddenly not seeing one of their idols anymore, after nonstop public exposure since the group became famous. After all, everyone knew where his creative partner John Lennon was – (this was the period when John was running around with new wife Yoko making headlines with outrageous stunts) – and Paul's absence from the spotlight stood out in comparison.

To the second point, the Paul-Is-Dead rumor made those believing the story feel good in the way that "Truthers" (people who believed 9/11 was an "inside government job") and "Birthers" (people who believed that Barack Obama wasn't born in the U.S.) felt good about their conspiracies – even though both those ideas are very distasteful concepts to many people. A fantastic story that seems to have a basis in actual ascertainable "facts" (shaky as those facts might be in reality) gets the listener excited; not only does it make sense of something strange, it also makes believers feel that *they're* in on a secret that has everyone else fooled, and, thus, they feel *smarter* than everyone else. They also feel part of an "inside group" - and that sense of belonging to an exclusive community makes them feel more important.

Primarily for those two reasons, a great story has the ability to "carry your brain away" – literally – through a concept that researchers call *"transportation."* Now, this isn't the kind of transportation that gets you to work or to the supermarket; *this* mode of transportation was discovered by researchers Melanie C. Green and Timothy C. Brock of Ohio State University[2] and it involves just how stories can impact your belief systems – even if those stories aren't necessarily factually accurate.

To quote the researchers, "...the reader loses access to some real-world facts in favor of accepting the narrative world that the author has created. This loss of access may occur on a physical level - a transported reader may not notice others entering the room, for example - or, more importantly, on a psychological level, a subjective distancing from reality. While the person is immersed in the story, he or she *may be less aware of real-world facts that contradict assertions made in the narrative."*

To put that in plain English, *a compelling story can be more important to someone than the facts.*

Want proof? Okay, check out the album cover from the last album the Beatles made together, *Abbey Road,* at the top of the following page:

---

2. Melanie C. Green and Timothy C. Brock, "The Role of Transportation in the Persuasiveness of Public Narratives," Journal of Personality and Social Psychology, Vol. 79, No. 5.

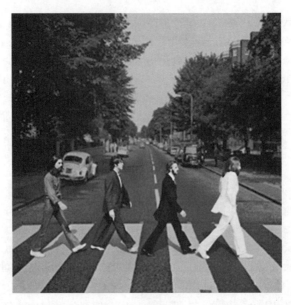

Now, you and I might look at that picture and say, "Hey, sure looks like Paul's alive to me – there he is, walking across the street with the other three Beatles. Hey, shouldn't he be able to afford a nice pair of loafers?"

But, when it came to those who had bought into the Paul-Is Dead conspiracy, here's what *they* saw: The four Beatles dressed to symbolize nothing less than a funeral procession, with John, dressed in white, as the minister, Ringo, dressed in black, as the undertaker, George, in denim jeans and shirt, as the gravedigger and Paul (or, more accurately, Mr. William Campbell, the guy who *looked* like Paul), barefoot and out of step with the others, as the corpse.

Oh, and that Volkswagen parked in the background? If you look closely, you'll see it has "28IF" as part of its license plate number – which, naturally to true Paul-Is-Dead conspiracy buffs, signified that Paul would have been 28 years old at that point - *if* he had lived.

In other words, all these obscure hidden meanings were more important to believers than the fact that *Paul was actually shown alive and well on the album cover.* And, since this was in an era that was well before Photoshop, it was pretty obvious that the photo was the real deal.

Again, this is just more evidence that the brain can't really distinguish between fact and fiction when a person has decided to buy into a story. As a matter of fact, it actively fights the impulse – because it's more important that *the brain defends the integrity of the story.*

This doesn't just apply to scurrilous dead Beatle stories. We all buy into narratives in our everyday lives – and when those narratives are challenged, we push back against the contradictions. How hard we push back depends on how invested we are in the particular story.

Think of someone who's a rabid Republican or Democrat who's confronted with information that contradicts his or her position. How many times have you said to yourself, when having a discussion with that kind of person, "This person is completely irrational – I have to stop arguing, there's no point!"

Odds are you're right. The person is being irrational – because the overall story he or she wants to believe in is more important than individual facts that conflict with it.

Getting back to the research of Green and Brock, the doctors discovered that it didn't matter if a story was presented as fact or fiction; if the story was compelling enough, if it had enough ability to "transport" people, it would directly impact their beliefs about the subject matter of the story.

And *that's* how someone could see Paul McCartney walking in a contemporary photograph – and still assume it was a big put-up job to send a hidden message about his death. In the words of Green and Brock, "Individuals may believe realistic fictional programs while discounting news reports that seem implausible."

As a matter of fact, that sounds a lot like our world today, doesn't it?

WHY STORIES WIN ARGUMENTS

Transportation is the ultimate goal for any good storyteller. And obviously, it should be the goal of a StorySelling effort as well.

Just as obviously, however, not just *any* story is going to prompt transportation (in later chapters in *StorySelling*, we're going to dig deeper into what ingredients are needed to create the kinds of story that enable this transformative process to happen).

What we want you to understand in *this* chapter, however, is that StorySelling is the most powerful tool you can use to communicate your personal brand and your company brand. All the research is very consistent on this fact (including the studies we've shared with you so far): ***stories are the best way to make your "argument."***

Why?

For the simple reason that the people hearing (or watching) the story…*don't perceive it as an argument.*

Instead, they identify with the leading character (providing he or she is likeable and interesting enough), put themselves in their shoes, feel what they feel and respond to what the story says about that person and the situation. They shut off the questioning part of their brain, as we've discussed, and give themselves over to the story's events and the consequences of those events.

And remember, since we do use stories to explain things, if we accept the narrative, then we will accept the conclusion. If the story is about how a murderer got away because of a court foul-up, we will feel more inclined to favor tougher laws. If the story is about how an innocent man is put on death row, we will feel more inclined to protect the rights of the accused. The story leads us to those ways of thinking not through direct persuasion, but by dramatic license.

We will only change or modify those beliefs so easily, however, *if we don't know an argument is being made.* To us, it's just a story; it's not supposed to mean anything beyond the beginning, middle and end of a tale. And that's how a story's so-called "moral" can sneak up on us and have an impact.

We use stories to process reality. Think about how powerful a statement that is. Think about how, whatever situation we find ourselves in, we must immediately concoct some kind of story to explain it, even though, ultimately, the story may be false. We still need to have something to hang onto until the "real story" is finally revealed.

StorySelling becomes invaluable when you want other people to process *your* reality in a memorable, effective way – the way you want them to see you.

Think about a trial lawyer doing his closing argument. How does he persuade the jury? Ninety-nine times out of a hundred, he'll frame what he wants the jury to believe in the form of a story – retelling the events crucial to the case in the way he wants them to be perceived.

In a sense, that's exactly what you do for yourself with StorySelling. You're telling a story about you and/or your business in the way you want them to perceive you. And because it's not seen as straight sales pitch, your audience's guard is significantly lowered and they're more willing to accept what you have to say.

THE VALUE OF AUTHENTICITY

We feel the need to end this chapter with a word about the truth.

This chapter may read as if stories are a license to lie – but there is great peril in that approach. Obviously, the Paul-Is-Dead conspiracy was pretty much dead and buried itself when Paul came out of hiding and began to give interviews. Whoever William Campbell might have been, he couldn't have been good enough to look exactly like Paul *and* sound exactly like Paul, unless someone was doing *Mission: Impossible* for real.

When a big lie is aggressively sold, it's only a matter of time before it does catch up with you. And with social media ready to blow the whistle at the drop of a hat and virally bust you, your window for successful deception is very short – as short as a few minutes, in some cases.

The fact is, even when your StorySelling is effective, your audience won't be as heavily invested in your narrative as they are in, say, their religion, their politics or their relationships. That means that, while you can achieve "transportation," it's still a tenuous ride that could be quickly derailed - *if* the story you're telling is ultimately a false one.

StorySelling offers you your best chance at reaching people on a deep, meaningful level that can genuinely motivate them to buy from you. Long term, however, you can't misuse that power – or it will come back to haunt you in ways you won't want to happen.

About JW

JW Dicks, Esq., is a Business Development Attorney, a Wall St. Journal, Best-Selling Author®—who has authored over 47 books—and a 2x Emmy® Award-winning Executive Producer.

JW is an XPrize Innovation Board member, Chairman of the Board of the National Academy of Best-Selling Authors®, Board Member of the National Association of Experts, Writers and Speakers® and Board Member of the International Academy of Film Makers®.

JW is the CEO of DNAgency, an Inc. 5000 Multi Media Company that represents over 2800 clients in 63 countries. He has been quoted on business and financial topics in national media such as *USA Today, The Wall Street Journal, Newsweek, Forbes, CNBC.com*, and *Fortune Magazine Small Business*.

Considered a Thoughtleader® and curator of information, JW has co-authored books with legends like Jack Canfield, Brian Tracy, Tom Hopkins, Dr. Nido Qubein, Steve Forbes, Richard Branson, Michael Gerber, Dr. Ivan Misner, and Dan Kennedy. He is the Publisher of *ThoughtLeader® Magazine*.

JW is called the "Expert to the Experts" and has appeared on business television Shows airing on ABC, NBC, CBS, and FOX affiliates around the country and coproduces and syndicates a line of franchised business television shows such as *Success Today, Wall Street Today, Hollywood Live, and Profiles of Success.*

JW and his wife of forty-seven years, Linda, have two daughters, four granddaughters, and two Yorkies. He is a sixth-generation Floridian and splits his time between his home in Orlando and his beach house on Florida's west coast.

About Nick

An Emmy Award-Winning Director and Producer, Nick Nanton, Esq., produces media and branded content for top thought leaders and media personalities around the world. Recognized as a leading expert on branding and storytelling, Nick has authored more than two dozen Best-Selling books (including the Wall Street Journal Best-Seller, *StorySelling*™) and produced and directed more than 50 documentaries, earning 5 Emmy wins and 18 nominations. Nick speaks to audiences internationally on the topics of branding, entertainment, media, business and storytelling at major universities and events.

As the CEO of DNA Media, Nick oversees a portfolio of companies including: The Dicks + Nanton Agency (an international agency with more than 3000 clients in 36 countries), Dicks + Nanton Productions, Ambitious.com and DNA Films. Nick is an award-winning director, producer and songwriter who has worked on everything from large scale events to television shows with the likes of Steve Forbes, Ivanka Trump, Sir Richard Branson, Rudy Ruettiger (inspiration for the Hollywood Blockbuster *"Rudy"*), Brian Tracy, Jack Canfield (*The Secret*, creator of the *Chicken Soup for the Soul* Series), Michael E. Gerber, Tom Hopkins, Dan Kennedy and many more.

Nick has been seen in *USA Today, The Wall Street Journal, Newsweek, BusinessWeek, Inc. Magazine, The New York Times, Entrepreneur®️ Magazine, Forbes, FastCompany*, and has appeared on ABC, NBC, CBS, and FOX television affiliates across the country as well as on CNN, FOX News, CNBC, and MSNBC from coast to coast.

Nick is a member of the Florida Bar, a member of The National Academy of Television Arts & Sciences (Home to the EMMYs), Co-founder of The National Academy of Best-Selling Authors®️, and serves on the Innovation Board of the XPRIZE Foundation, a non-profit organization dedicated to bringing about "radical breakthroughs for the benefit of humanity" through incentivized competition, best known for its Ansari XPRIZE which incentivized the first private space flight and was the catalyst for Richard Branson's Virgin Galactic. Nick also enjoys serving as an Elder at Orangewood Church, working with Young Life, Downtown Credo Orlando, Entrepreneurs International and rooting for the Florida Gators with his wife Kristina and their three children, Brock, Bowen and Addison.

Learn more at:

- www.NickNanton.com
- www.CelebrityBrandingAgency.com

CHAPTER 15

VISION

BY COLLEEN CRAWFORD

What is the single most strategic component of any individual, relationship or organization?

VISION

What is VISION? "To imagine the future with imagination or wisdom, a mental image of what the future will or could be like."

What exactly does that mean? Why is that important?

When I was first introduced to this concept in 1998, it was hard for me to get my head wrapped around it. However, I was enlightened by the amazing Kathy Ollerton in a training on victim/responsibility consciousness. I was at that time, by all outside appearances, a happily married, top-producing Realtor, fit and healthy, mother of three, making plenty of money. However, behind closed doors, I was miserable in a failing marriage, working 60+ hours a week while a nanny was raising my children. I was lonely, stressed out and resentful. I truly believed I was stuck and it was so and so's fault.

At the age of 33, I learned I AM the result of my thinking, not my circumstances. I didn't "have to" live this life, I was "choosing" this life, and more importantly, literally creating my unhappy circumstances with my thinking process. Wow! I never realized how my focus on all the negative in my life was actually creating more of it! This new awareness inspired me to consciously craft a positive VISION for the life that I did want.

I GOT TO WORK!

Napoleon Hill said "To Think Is To Create" meaning that all results in anyone's life are a manifestation of the mind. That may sound "woo woo" to some people, however, I will soon demonstrate how this is true.

The first step in any Vision work, be it personal or professional, is to responsibly own the current results. We cannot get from point A to point B, unless we clearly define point A. The next step is to get clear on Point B. Here are a few simple steps to get the juices flowing:

1. Look BACKWARD

Pretend you are at your funeral, and someone is in the front of the room reading your eulogy. What are they saying about you? How did you live your life? What impact did you make on people, your family, this world? What is your legacy? What did your business provide for people, for this world? Much of the population takes their hopes, goals and dreams to their grave. This is an exercise in awareness. What have you created thus far, and what do you want the rest of your life to look like?

2. Look FORWARD

Pretend you have a personal Genie that will grant you whatever you want, give yourself permission to go BIG. More than 80% of the people and businesses I work with have never worked on their Vision. I give two assignments: create a bucket list of everything they want to "Be, Do, Have and Give" in their lifetime, and write down what they want to create in the next 12 months.

When was the last time you took time to visualize your life 12 months, 3 years or 5 years from now? I find most people live day by day without any defined future, mostly because they do not understand their own inherent power to create it.

There is a saying, "A man without a vision for his future always returns to his past" and this is true. Success starts with awareness, taking ownership of all current results, then clearly defining the ideal future state. Otherwise, we keep doing what we have always done and keep getting what we have always gotten!

> *Ownership is to be responsible, and to be*
> *responsible is personal power!*

Countless people give away their personal power by blaming themselves, blaming events, blaming other people or the world for their lack of success, whatever success means to them. We can take back our personal power by becoming aware of how we created our results in the first place. With awareness that we are the causal agent of our happiness, love, success, health and wealth, it can be exciting and powerful to craft and commit to a VISION. Below are identifiable steps as to how this actually happens. I call these the Chain of Success and the Chain of Failure, each demonstrating how one single thought (goal) can translate into two different results.

CHAIN OF SUCCESS IS: T B I E A B C R

1) We have an inspired **Thought**.
2) We have a **Belief** system that filters that thought.
3) All humans think in pictures, so the thought attaches to associated **Imagery** – internal and external.
4) The imagery generates **Emotion**.
5) Emotions spawn **Attitude** and **Behavior**.
6) Behavior is revealed in **Choice**.

7) Choice becomes **RESULTS**.

Example of Success:

Thought (Goal):	I want to lose ten pounds.
Belief System:	I can do this, I have done it before!
Imagery:	I VISUALIZE myself, imagining my body 10 pounds lighter, comfortably fitting into my favorite jeans.
Emotion:	I am excited to get into those jeans!
Attitude:	YAY! It's going to be a healthy day!
Behavior:	I eagerly plan my diet and workouts.
Choice:	I eat 1400 calories a day, workout 3x a week and drink more water.

RESULT: I lose ten pounds.

CHAIN OF FAILURE IS THE SAME: T B I E A B C R

Example of Failure:

Thought (Goal):	I want to lose ten pounds.
Belief System:	UGH! Doubtful I can do this, it's hard!
Imagery:	All I SEE is that ugly fat in the mirror, and my muffin top flowing over the edges of my jeans.
Emotion:	I am sad and depressed, nothing fits.
Attitude:	Ugh!! This sucks, I hate dieting.
Behavior:	I stall on planning, complain about the diet, the food, everything.
Choice:	I skip the gym, accept my hubby's invite to the couch with a bag of Oreo's and a bottle of wine.

RESULT: I gain ten pounds.

What's to notice? Same thought, same goal, same chain, different result. Notice we are literally ONE thought away from success! This chain applies to ANY thought, whether losing ten pounds, gaining ten new clients, taking a trip to Italy, finding the love of your life, increasing company profit 20%, making the college basketball team, etc.

The great news? *If we can create a chain of failure, then we can create a chain of success!* The shift must take place in our belief system. VISION, as the single most strategic component in life, is one tool that can drastically shift results. The key is this, we CAN control our thoughts, we can specifically create and control imagery, and we can use our imagination to support the end result we want.

All thoughts translate through this process. The only difference between professional and personal Vision, is how many human beings, how many minds, need to be in alignment with the Vision. Getting an entire organization committed to a VISION is power; it's not added power, it's multiplier power. A company that aligns its employees with the company Vision will fast track goals and manifest success immeasurably faster than without.

Back up for a minute, I do not believe in the word failure. Life is life, and all of life is one experience after another. Our personal judgment may call an experience a failure, yet, how does that serve us? Placing negative energy on experiences in our life will not assist us in moving to our desired future ideal state. Instead of labeling mistakes or undesired results as failures, how about considering them "opportunities to learn and grow?"

There are many "learning and growth opportunities" in divorce, failing health, or a bankrupt business. Focusing on the negative destroys the present moment, and worse yet, imagining it with emotion brings more of it into your future. Embrace what was effective, let go of what was ineffective. Placing focus on mistakes is a waste of precious mind space and hijacks our brilliance from learning the lesson and moving to solution orientation.

Here's something to note:
- What we focus on expands.
- Where our attention goes, energy flows.
- What we think about, dwell on, focus on, visualize in our minds, say to ourselves over and over is not describing our now, it is **prescribing our future**.
- Pay attention: focusing on the negative, or what didn't work, or what isn't working, ultimately creates more of it.

Zig Ziglar says: "Worry is negative goal setting!" and he is right.

Instead of the downward spiral, how about focusing on an upward spiral? That is VISION. Purposefully think about, dwell on, focus on, place attention on, in thoughts, imagery, emotions and words, what you WANT to create in your life. Get excited! VISION is a channeling tool for the Laws of Attraction. If we are clear and committed to "what we want", the abundant universe will deliver; it always does. Thoughts are things. Everything in life started as a thought: the chair you sit in, the light in your room, asking someone on a date, the workout you did or didn't do today and the savings account you opened or didn't open. Everything starts with a thought.

If you want to change results on the outside, you must get to work on the inside. We have 60 to 80 thousand thoughts a day! Wouldn't it be interesting to investigate what percentage of thoughts are spent on negative self-talk, what's not working, failures of the past and/or fear of the future? Imagine the possibilities if sixty thousand thoughts a day were excited about your future ideal state!

You don't need to focus on the 'how it will happen', the 'how' is the domain of the universe. The Laws of Attraction are like gravity, you may not see them, however, they are always working. Your Vision, intention and attention activate and harness the

Laws of Attraction. You can learn more about the science behind the Laws of Attraction by watching a movie called *The Secret* and reading Napoleon Hills's book *Think and Grow Rich*.

Commit to your Vision and believe it is possible.

Visionaries make the impossible, possible. So can YOU!

Bottom line:

Thoughts, Imagery, Emotions, Attitude, Behavior and Choices are ALL within our control.

Visionaries like Walt Disney, MLK, JFK, Steve Jobs, Oprah, Jim Carey, Jack Canfield, Lindsay Vonn, Arnold Schwarzenegger, Michael Jordan and countless others used the power of Visualization to create their ideal future state. Mental imagery and visualization exercises have been common practice and scientifically proven with professional, collegiate and Olympian athletes for decades.

We can choose to focus on the past, lamenting over our mistakes, and place our attention on all that is "not" working, or, we can choose to be visionaries and *Focus on the Vision, not the current condition*. Imagine and emotionalize your ideal future state, and no matter the obstacles, commit to making your ideas and dreams real. Be open, pay attention, and notice signals from the universe. As your focus expands and energy increases, forces will align to deliver resources to fulfill your Vision.

Do not take your ideas and dreams to the graveyard!

Get clear. Get excited! Craft your VISION statement, make a Vision board, develop a personal mantra, do whatever it takes to shift your belief system into knowing you have the power to make your impossible, possible.

Do not leave this wonderful opportunity called LIFE, to chance.

Get URGENT, activate your WILL TO WIN,
and create the life you deserve!

About Colleen

Colleen Crawford is a Coach and Trainer passionately committed to impacting and improving the lives of others. Her specialties include Vision, Breakthrough, and Goal-Getting programs as well as custom corporate programs and events.

With a vast array of transition and change under her belt, including two divorces, single motherhood, three grown children, five states, 27 moves, 16 schools, 22 surgeries and 31 companies, she has countless effective AND ineffective experiences in life. This provides her a uniquely qualified depth in understanding people/businesses who are struggling and unable to see their way to the other side.

Her 23 years in all aspects of real estate in Ohio, Nevada, Colorado and California include: sales, management and coaching. Mindset was key to success for her clients, hence, her immersion in personal growth and self-improvement work.

Colleen is a graduate of more than 20 life-improvement programs including Anthony Robbins Leadership Academy, KO Productions Summit, Fire, Inspire, Brian Tracy Success Academy, Jack Canfield Success Principles, Personal Success Institute Basic Seminar, Life Success Course, Pacesetter Leadership Dynamic, Women's Leadership Seminar, NLP, Higher Consciousness Studies/ Primordial Meditation with Deepak Chopra, Dr. Demartini's Breakthrough Experience, Keller Williams University Quantum Leap, Train the Trainer, National Academy of Sports Medicine and more.

Failure is not a word in her book; life is a journey of experiences without judgment. With extensive education in so many life-improvement programs, she has a unique portfolio of skills, tools and programs to assist with personal transformation.

Her astute and intuitive sense coupled with proven methodology is her recipe for successful transformative training. Whether personal or professional, she crafts an experiential path for clients to assess themselves in truth, release ineffective thought patterns and behaviors, and embrace their extraordinary leadership capabilities for personal empowerment.

Colleen happily lives her purpose fulfilling her VISION year after year, creating new results verifying the strategy, validity and success of Vision work. Married to Dan Barnett, with five amazing young adults, Christa, Matt, Mike, Nick and Sammi, her personal interests include documentaries, meditation, holistic healing, fitness, anything educational and inspirational, the great outdoors, road cycling, boxing, golf, traveling, the ocean, and love of people.

You can find her at:

- www.colleencrawford.com
- https://www.linkedin.com/in/colleenbcrawford/

CHAPTER 16

THE DREAM IS REAL

BY HARRY OGLETREE

"If you could write the script to your own life, what would you write? I decided I could not quit, I had too much to live for. If I possessed nothing else, I had a glimmer of HOPE. I was still alive! That meant something, didn't it? Questions from the past like, "Don't you ever fight for anything you want?" What had happened to my fighting spirit, my unconquerable will, my desire to live life to the fullest? I was 43 years old and felt stuck. If only I could just move a little bit. Yes, I needed ACTION. I love my children very much. I often wonder if they know that. I must try. I simply must do something with my life, but what?"

After penning these words, I sat down and prayerfully wrote out my gut level honest dreams! What I didn't tell you is that I had given up a good job that I worked at for 14 years. I moved to a new city and the new job did not work out. I was behind on child support. I was behind on rent. My mother had just passed away and I was unfaithful in serving my Lord. I labored intently and arduously alone in my half-furnished apartment. These words comforted me, "Have faith and do your best at what you are doing now. I can earn money immediately and get started again. Yes, I am starting again."

One of the greatest and most liberating ideas in life is when a person realizes they have options. We always have options. We might have to relocate, enhance or learn new skills, yet we always have options! As I began searching for my options, I looked in the mirror and asked myself that age-old question, "What would I do with my life if time and money were not an issue?" I gave myself the freedom to dream again! I had the time and it didn't cost a dime to sit down and record my dreams. That's when I realized that staring back at me was both the problem and the solution. It was all up to me, regardless of what others have or have not done.

I had nothing left to defend. The only thing that I had worth fighting for was my future. I listed, as best I could, my dream life. I started with what was most important to me, my own personal development program. It was designed to enhance the health of my Mental, Physical, Emotional and Spiritual states. My relationship with my Lord was paramount. Second, I penned my dream relationship with my children. Third, I penned what my dream relationship with my future wife would look like, even though I admitted I needed a girlfriend first! Fourth, I penned my dream career, earning potential and eventual financial freedom. Fifth, I penned what my dream wardrobe, automobile, and future home would look like. I even penned my dream vacation in Hawaii that I had failed to take my mother on! As I labored on this life-altering project I did not share its content with anyone. I only prayed about it to my God and Father.

I was slowly regaining a sense of purpose and energized hope in my life. I read it every morning and every evening and carried note cards in my pocket, refreshing my memory and rejuvenating my vision of my future often during the day. I wrote all my dreams out in the affirmative as though they had already happened.

Since I was broke, I went to the public library and secured a library card. Did you know that your library can get almost any book you desire to read even if they have to send to another library to procure it? Not to mention all the learning CDs, DVDs and Blue-rays that are available?

I have learned the hard way that you only share your dreams and aspirations with people who want it for you as much as you would want it for them! Most will not understand your dreams initially. Yet, why should they? They are your dreams! Having said that, take note that one conversation with the right person or persons can change your destiny. There is no substitute for a good mentor if you are fortunate enough to have one or more than one. When I mentioned my Self Development program earlier, I meant I am very selective in who and what I read and listen to. I am more selective in what I attend. People with knowledge are worth their weight in gold. I heard or read many years ago that if you would read one hour a day in your area of expertise, in three years you would know more than most people on that subject. I have read a minimum of one hour every day since.

My Will to Win initially came from my desire to move away from that which I did not want and move towards that which I did want, because of the promises that I made to myself and others. The Will to Win seems to come from that which pushes us and that which pulls us. What we don't want pushes us and what we do want pulls us. Exposure of what we could be or have by experience, observation or study will strengthen our will also. People who believe in you and encourage you should be treasured. Sometimes a kind word or nudge from a stranger can be just what is needed to get you to the next step.

Once a person really decides what they want in life and know why they want it, it is simply a matter of when and figuring out how and with whom! I say simply, not because it is easy, but because what motivates us personally will make all the difference in the world. When we know 'what' and 'why', it literally allows us to see clearly what is important and what is not. That which takes us nearer to our dreams is important and that which takes us away from our dreams is to be avoided at all cost! The tough question in life, as we grow older, is not usually what is right or wrong. In reality, it's the ability to distinguish between what is good and what is the best for what we are trying to achieve or how we want to live, that counts.

Dreams come alive when we create them, write them down, visualize them and pursue them with passion. Selecting as many avenues as you can to portray your dreams will ultimately create a strong desire to bring them to fruition. Brochures, books, movies, visitations, test drives, etc., will all help in creating a strong vision, yet one of your most profound aides will be your very own imagination. Try to imagine only the desired result or at least overcoming the challenges that stand between you and your dreams. One of the most profound ways to intensify your Will to Win is to couple your dreams with self-selected music.

Dreams and aspirations will allow you to have a strong will. Only concrete goals, leading from where you are to your dreams, will propel you to Win! The Will to Win is really our commitment to successfully performing the necessary tasks skillfully on a regular basis. Execution of skills is the life blood of maintaining the will to win until victory has been won. When you execute a skillset and earn a desired result, remember to reward yourself. Make sure the reward is predetermined and is consistent with keeping balance as you build your dreams one activity at a time. You only enjoy the reward when you achieve the desired result!

The single thread that propelled my learning curve in creating and maintaining my Will to Win was discovering and discussing the power of ideas and thoughts and implementing them into my own life – where they grew into habits and skills. For many, this will be over simplification, however, on one side of my note cards I wrote out my desired activity and on the flip side I wrote why I was doing it and the eventual earned reward.

Ultimately my Will to Win has grown through my faith in God. Because of Jesus, I want to be all that I can be in all areas of my life. Integrity is the oxygen of all relationships and joined purposes. My hope and desire is that in some small way you may be encouraged in your Will to Win by my message. Go forward! Take a single step in the direction of your dreams and you will alter the course of humanity, not to mention your own life. Action is creation.

It will not be easy. If it was, everyone would be doing it! I have a question for you… Your family has been preparing for a vacation for over a year. Everyone is on board and you are joyfully driving down the road miles from home and you get a flat tire. What do you do? You know exactly what you do. FIX IT AND GET ON DOWN THE ROAD! There will be challenges and struggles. My advice to you is FIX THEM AND GET ON DOWN THE ROAD. Your Dreams are expecting you.

I am now 60 years old, happily married and we spent our honeymoon in Kauai. We currently live in the home my wife dreamed of as a child. I have a wonderful relationship with my children. I am serving my Lord faithfully. Thirty-four years later I returned to my alma mater and earned my BA degree in Bible. I promised my mother I would. I also had the privilege to serve as Chaplain on our son's basketball team at the same University, Ohio Valley University. I give my Lord all the glory, praise and thanks.

I leave you with a poem. It is called……

Woolly Bear

> Crawl Woolly Bear Crawl
> Crawl upon the dirt
> Crawl Woolly Bear Crawl
> Crawl for you must
> Crawl Woolly Bear Crawl
> For one day you shall Fly!

How to Create a Strong Will to Win/The Dream is Real

1. Access your situation.
2. Realize you have options.
3. Give yourself the Freedom to Dream.

4. Create Your Dream List in all Areas of Your Life:
   a. Spiritual
   b. Family
   c. Health
   d. Career
   e. Self-Development
   f. Homes, Automobiles and Wardrobes
   g. Vacations, etc.
5. Write it out and Read it often, Visualizing your Desired Outcome with the help of brochures, visitations, etc.
6. Determine Why this is very Important to You.
7. Only Share these Dreams with Key People in your Life.
8. Start where you are as you head towards your Dreams.
9. Take Action and Keep Growing.
10. Reward Your Achievements.
11. Remember The Dream is Real.

About Harry

Harry Ogletree is the President of Golden Bridge Greetings, a company created to encourage those struggling and those succeeding. Through the written, spoken and visual word, Golden Bridge Greetings strives to provide success principles and ideas to encourage you to be your best in all areas of your life!

PS 118:24

Contact Information:

- 740-336-2516 cell
- Harryo.6wcofc@gmail.com

CHAPTER 17

I BELIEVE IN MIRACLES: FOUR THINGS THAT CHANGED MY LIFE

BY JESÚS P. CALDERÓN

When I was young, I hoped my future would be full of adventure and new ideas, but somewhere on the way I was derailed. I was plagued with constant thoughts about my life being "over," despite there being no cause for harm around me. What was happening to me? It was a period of invisible causes – a time of anxiety and a lack of hope. The things I loved were disappearing from sight, one by one.

It would be unfair to take you on that journey, to know what it felt like to feel as though I was refusing to breathe by refusing to live. But I can take you on the journey out of it, and where I am at now. I learned a great many things during this difficult time. Of course, the highs and lows were a part of my road to come back to myself. My gratitude for this learning opportunity cannot be measured.

This trying time allowed me the opportunity to ask myself what it was that I really wanted. In finding my purpose, I learned more about myself and what motivated me. I also grew to appreciate the many things I had. With the passing of time, and a great amount of work, I have been given the greatest gift: my life, to do with it what I will. And so, I asked myself: how can I help others? How can I be of service? How can I pass on this wisdom so that others don't have to know the suffering I experienced?

I believe that miracles happen. I am living proof. I now regard these insights as some of the greatest blessings that life has given me. I acknowledge the good fortune I experienced in returning to health, and it is now my life's work to share that gift with others. My greatest desire is to be but a grain of sand that contributes to the world with a connection to ourselves – to our inner power.

In this chapter, I will share with you four things that changed my life forever. Pay close attention to these lessons and look for ways to apply them into your own life and practice. It is important that you enjoy the adventure of getting to know yourself and discover what you can learn from introspection. Learn to listen to the secrets you keep inside. While these four pillars are invisible, it's best to think of them as seeds: with nourishment and time, you can create deep roots and permanence. These lessons are important for inner knowledge, inner peace, and to create the fullest future and health we desire.

Finally, before reading further, it's important to remember that using any of these tools and lessons will be responsible for active changes in your day to day. These lessons will change you, and help connect your desires, hopes, and dreams. It's easy to say that you will no longer be the same as when you first started, but it is also good to remember, as with any motivational work, understand that you are your own master. I believe these lessons will work for you as they have worked for me.

I. <u>The Miracle of the Invisible World</u>

There are miracles all around us, we just have to teach ourselves to open up to see them. To understand how to see miracles around us, I recommend taking time to look within, as well as practice being present.

There is vulnerability in looking deep inside of oneself. I remember feeling as though I was on a journey to the center of the earth – it was such a narrow, deep, and uncomfortable path. Learning to let myself go and be present meant I also had to learn to leave the ego behind – to leave my desires and worries, to surrender and let go, and also to overcome. By looking within and truly seeing life for the miracle it is, I found the monk, the sage, and the guide who lives in me. Each one of these personas was hidden, just waiting for discovery. I believe we all have these inside us. Turning off the outside lights frees you to light up inside.

Today I know that this path and techniques can be taught to others. Part of the work I do is connecting others with the capacity for connecting to this inner place, one of abundance and peace. This inner place already lives inside of each of us! In my experience, people feel a difference immediately—a serenity in discovering their truths. This inner place is available to us all, and free for you to return to whenever you need a place of calm and peace.

You might ask yourself how to access something that already exists inside of you, but that you haven't previously connected to. The first step to finding it sounds simple, but is some of the most important work you can do.

Practice Being Present

Perhaps you have heard of letting go – the act of living in the present moment. There is an element of childlike peace to this mental state. To achieve it, you must resolve to leave the ego (and all things of adulthood) behind. The path is simple and innate but does demand both your time and your focus in order to experience the benefits.

The practice of Meditation and Mindfulness were the first steps that I took. And it is part of what I now practice and teach.

The way I began this process was to observe my breathing. By focusing on inhalation and exhalation, you have the ability to present in your body in a tangible way. Try taking a few moments to observe your own breathing patterns, deeply in and out. While you do so, close your eyes. Repeat the following thoughts in your mind, or say them softly aloud if you are in an open space to do so:

> *There is only one here and now.*
> *There is no future nor concern.*
> *There is no past or burdens.*

Take a few moments every day to add this mindfulness into your daily routine.

Some other approaches to this practice include walking in nature, giving thanks for what you have, or hugging loved ones. Ask yourself: What have been the moments that I have felt peace, harmony, and health? Access these truths and revisit them in tranquil, private times. Learn from you: in your own heart dwells the master and the answers you seek.

II. <u>The Purpose of Life</u>

Sometimes it is necessary to close your eyes in order to open them and awaken to a fresh start. When you take everything away, we are free to see what is really important. For many who have trauma or major life events, it puts their life in perspective, and asks questions they might have previously been uncomfortable to ask.

For me, my starting over helped me identify my purpose in life. There were a few questions that helped me move in the right direction. For this exercise, take a piece of paper and write down the questions that you most wish to answer. Note that the ones that are the most difficult, or uncomfortable, are likely the ones you most need to answer during your introspective journey.

Ask Yourself Important Questions

- *If you were granted one wish, who would you be, what would you be doing?*
- *What job would create the most satisfaction?*
- *Where would you go on holiday?*
- *What are the most important stories of your life?*
- *What do you really want, and what values do you honor with these desires?*

Write down your answers and come back to those that are the most difficult to answer. As you identify your values, you can create a powerful metaphor that will motivate and inspire you. There are many ways to discover your purpose, and it is one of life's greatest joys that we get to adventure and explore.

Of course, know that your answers may change over time, or as more is discovered on your journey. Remember that this kind of work is never really done, and practice self-compassion and care as you dig deep into your heart's desires and values.

Strive to live life to the fullest in honor of your values, but let life take you on the journey that is destined for you!

III. Beliefs Create Reality

Beliefs are seeds; the fruits will depend on the seed you planted and the effort you expend. Ask yourself: what fruits do you want to have? Seek out the seeds that best support you, provide nourishment, and that thrive in your environment.

Beliefs can create our reality and steer our future. This is a fundamental principle in so many disciplines of knowledge, from religions to philosophies to institutions. We have the power to create our own reality, as well as steer our ways of feeling, seeing life, and relating to others. While the methods all vary, there are overlapping principles that are proven to work.

I teach some of these frameworks in my courses. These are structured for success and fulfillment, and I truly believe in them as I have seen them help others.

The Three Beliefs To Begin:

1. **Yes, You Can**. Anything is possible. Every time you think something is possible, a change in your brain's disposition gives room for this new possibility. The belief you can influence and steer your life will empower you. Free yourself from the constraints of negativity and self-doubt by thinking positively and constructively. Put your mind to accomplishing your dreams and you will be able to!

2. **Everything is Learning**. Life is a path, not a destiny. Life is a journey, not a destination. Today, I can see backwards and realize that I cannot count my failures without also acknowledging all that I learned. Life is always trying to teach us something. If you are in a difficult situation today, train yourself to gain perspective in each situation. Remember that a challenge is there to teach and strengthen you. In doing so, you are guaranteed to get the best version of yourself.

3. **Show Gratitude**. There's absolutely always something to be thankful for. Remember to take time to appreciate the little things and give thanks whenever you can. Showing gratitude can be infectious and can set off a chain of positive reactions. In my own life, acknowledging this has led me to a state of appreciation

and gratitude that attracts more of that which I truly want. I believe in the law of attraction; my biochemistry changes every time I acknowledge this, opening me up for new opportunities and appreciation.

Beliefs have the amazing power to mold and create our reality! This means that the reality that you want is in direct relation to the beliefs that you must cultivate and continue to nurture. You have all the tools you need already in place!

IV. <u>Courage & The Will To Win</u>

By now you have a good idea of the ways you can manifest your own miracles in your life. Sure, each of us has the power and the courage inside. All we have to do is access this power. However, the bigger question is this: how do we get the courage and drive that pushes us forward? How do we have the will it takes to win?

In my experience, this is a constant process. But there are steps that can unlock your own potential and the courage that is already innate in you...if you are willing to put in the effort it takes to do so.

Certainly, you can use your pain or dissatisfaction to move you forward. This is human nature: we push past things that make us uncomfortable in order to get to the other side. However, you do not have to go through adversity, great struggle, or even hit rock-bottom to access the courage it takes to persevere.

Since this section relies heavily on human nature, what best to show us who we really are than to look to us at our most simple state: as infants.

The Baby

If you have ever watched a baby start to get uncomfortable, you know how quickly a passing thought moves to action that involves his entire body. Perhaps this baby becomes so uncomfortable that he begins to cry, but then he escalates to loud wailing, writhing as if in indecipherable pain. Within only a few moments, the child has gone from discomfort to living in a devastating reality.

Perhaps he only wants his bottle, but what we know about infants is how their wants and desires involve their whole body and all senses. Crying is a way to harmonize dissent, and to communicate wordlessly.

We deal with all kinds of situations we dislike, but as we grow into adults, we learn to communicate, to weigh circumstances based on severity, and to react (think of flight or flight). My advice is to think back on the courage it takes to express what we really want as soon as we know we want it. Like the baby who is hungry, and only knows how to express it with action and sound.

Use the following three steps as an exercise to create space in your imagination:

1. Live your situation intensely as a baby does. Increase the experience, amplify the images that come to your mind – of sounds, sensations, and thoughts.
2. Observe what your future looks like if you do not make any changes in your life. Think about what would happen if you do not act or move. Consider all the possible details to make this fantasy feel like a reality...one that you do not want to take hold but are not actively steering.
3. Clear your thoughts and think again about what your future would be like if you took the first step today towards what you really want. How you would feel? What are all the details that you can plan for? Take the good with the bad in this first step: acknowledge the risks and the successes.

Use dissatisfaction, pain, or discomfort as your strength and courage to move. Life is learning, and everything is possible when you put your mind to it.

Finally, reflect back on the other lessons in this chapter. Remember to practice mindfulness, ask yourself important questions, and give yourself space to grow and evolve!

The best way to enjoy this path begins from within ourselves. We have the power and strength to create our own destinies from the center of the universe – the universe that you inhabit. Don't be afraid to steer towards that which you truly want. You have the ability to make changes, and the world is full of possibilities. Life is exciting! It's a road, an adventure, and most importantly: it's whatever you want it to be. Miracles happen. I'm convinced that we create miracles...even if *we are the miracle.*

About Jesús

Jesús P. Calderón is a visionary, a writer, a teacher, and a lover. He sees the strength of the human experience and the value in learning from the simplest things. Jesús values time spent in nature, where meditation and mindfulness have become an essential part of his daily life.

His formal educational background includes electronic systems engineering and a Master's Degree in Business Administration. However, open-mindedness and an emphasis on diversity of thought gave Jesús the freedom to discover himself through studies in various other subjects. He attended classes in Neuro-linguistic programming, where he received certification in neuro-linguistic programming and Health, with the aim of improving lives and instruction for others who were looking to make changes in their lives. In addition, Jesús became certified in Yoga, meditation, and Ayurveda from the Chopra Center University. He is also fluent in Spanish.

It took a life lesson to change Jesús P. Calderón's life. After restoring his physical and mental health, Jesús was set on a spiritual path towards a broader state of consciousness and happiness.

Today, Jesús is passionate about creating learning experiences and bringing healing, joy and resources to people to live a better life. He offers courses and workshops that include meditation, mindfulness, neuro-linguistic programming, and other disciplines in order to build a life of miracles and goodwill.

Open and happy, Jesús P. Calderón identifies strongly with an appreciation of life's challenges and hurdles, while remembering to always believe in miracles and show gratitude. His teachings and many writings support this philosophy, which he hopes to share with those who need it most.

Jesús hopes to continue to make a difference on this planet, by connecting others with their innate ability to believe in themselves, heal, and create.

Contact information for Jesús:

- Website: jesuscalderoni.com
- Instagram: @jesuscalderoni
- Facebook: @JesusPCalderoni
- Email: info@jesuscalderoni.com

CHAPTER 18

HARNESSING THE POWER OF THE MIND, TO WIN

BY STEPHANIE CALDOW

I hope you're sitting down as the following statement is likely to hit you right between the eyes...

Everything that you have or don't have in your life (both positive and negative) in the areas of health, wealth and lifestyle is the result of who you have been 'being', and the subsequent repercussions of the choices that you have made along life's journey.

As controversial as this statement may appear, let's examine the underlying truth behind it. There are an abundance of factors that influence the achievement of your goals in life; in this chapter we'll focus on the ones that are within your control – your mindset, beliefs, habits and goal-setting systems.

For many years, I never understood the impact my mindset, behaviour and choices had on my life. I tried to be the best person that I could, I treated others as I would like to be treated and so on... The facts were that I wasn't getting the results that I desired. Challenging personal and professional situations continued to occur.

I didn't realise it then, however, I had scripted my entire life story when I was a child. When I five years old, I tried to protect my baby sister from a bully. When I couldn't stop the situation, I created the story that 'I wasn't enough', and 'the world was a scary place where bad stuff happens'. I tucked away this narrative in my subconscious and carried it with me like a warm blanket. Every decision that I made thereafter was playing on the back of this tune. Every outcome that I achieved, whether positive or negative, would further validate my story. No wonder I wasn't achieving the results I was looking for, my brain was sabotaging my success!

> *We see the world not as it really is, but as we are.*
> ~ Anais Nin

While we may not be aware of it, we all have a narrative that plays via our internal dialogue (that little voice in our head). The brain used to utilise this function to keep us safe from dinosaurs (part of the flight-or-fight function), however, there aren't too many roaming the streets these days, so the messages we receive are more along the lines of "Danger, love ahead – we know how that turned out last time. Run for your life!" (Fear of being hurt.) Or, "Caution, you're moving outside of your comfort zone, this is unknown territory – you don't really want to achieve that goal, do you?" (Fear of failure or even success.)

Our beliefs act as filters through which we see the world. Imagine that every morning when you wake, you put on your 'belief glasses'; your experiences throughout the day (both positive and negative) are then influenced by your specific point of view (POV). We were not born with beliefs about money, worthiness, intelligence, etc., so what happened? Your POV is a combination of your beliefs – made up of your past experiences – and influences from friends, family, teachers and media. Exposure to repetitious messages causes our brain to develop and reinforce neural pathways and connections that retain them as stories or beliefs about ourselves and the world around us. These in turn directly influence our default thoughts and behavioural responses, and the results achieved to this point. When we run this internal dialogue often enough, they become belief systems – things that we accept to be true. These in turn affect our mindset – the way that we think.

Prominent psychologist Carol Dweck's research suggests that mindset is based upon self-perception. Fixed mindset people believe that their basic qualities of intelligence and talent are fixed traits, they don't require effort. Growth mindset people believe that basic abilities can be developed through hard work and dedication, failure is seen as a lesson to the path of understanding and goal achievement. People are often unaware of their mindsets, even though they have a huge impact on all facets of life.

Individuals with a fixed mindset often limit themselves and their achievements. They tell themselves stories such as, "I'm hopeless at math, playing sport, or being in a relationship, etc." They would rather not try (and therefore not achieve), than try and fail, which would prove that they're not as naturally talented as people perceive them to be. Instead they remain within the safety of their comfort zone *where their results are predictable.*

Alternatively, a growth viewpoint appreciates that our brains and talent are just the basic tools for us to work with. In order to accomplish anything, these tools need to be developed. This perspective creates a desire for learning and a resilience that is essential in having the will to win – personally or professionally.

We are in fact a combination of both mindsets, the key is to notice which one you are in most often. Max Maltz said, "you can never outperform your own self-image." If your story is, *"I'm a failure", "I'm unlovable"* or *"I'm not enough"* and *"I can't go through a situation like 'that' again,"* you'll live a very constricted life based on the fear of potential pain.

When you realise that you have a fixed mindset about something, create the possibility of a new story and way of being. You can start with looking at the basics: you know what? I'm proficient at walking these days. It was only due to practice that I became so skilled. There was a time when I used to fall, but I persisted (hundreds of times) until I nailed it!

Experts don't keep going until they get it right, they keep going until they can't get it wrong.
~ Dr. Sarah McKay

These days we are so used to being comfortable that we often quit before we really get started; for comfort is the killer of motivation. Could you do as Thomas Edison did and 'fail' 10,000 times? In his famous quote, he said, *"I have not failed, I've just found 10,000 ways that won't work."* Michael Jordan was also inspirational in his consistent focus and discipline in the face of failure and defeat. *"I've missed more than 9,000 shots in my career. I've lost almost 300 games. Twenty-six times, I've been trusted to take the game-winning shot and missed. I've failed over and over and over again in my life. And that is why I succeed."* Both Jordan and Edison realised that failure is just 'feedback' that we can use to better ourselves or a situation. Every time we try something we receive feedback and can adjust the process accordingly for our next attempt.

Habits are another sphere that play a major role in the achievement of our goals. Over 90% of what you think and do is habitual. If we had to think about every minute task such as brushing our teeth and tying our shoelaces, we would quickly become exhausted. Habits ensure that we can complete tasks on autopilot so that we can devote mental energy elsewhere. However, while this mechanism ensures the brains energy resources aren't depleted too quickly, this can often result in 'mindlessness' (completing tasks without question or awareness). This too can lead to behaviours that aren't conducive to achieving your goals.

STRUCTURE OF A HABIT

1. TRIGGER – Triggers can be external or internal. They switch your brain into automatic.
2. BEHAVIOUR – These can be positive or destructive, through action or inaction.
3. REWARD – An emotional benefit.

Every habit has a purpose that serves you. They are often so challenging to break because they are undertaken at an unconscious level. To take control of your habits you need to recognise them, then understand their triggers, behaviours and rewards.

Examples of triggers include:

- Location – a bar, where your subsequent behaviour is drinking alcohol
- Emotional state – feeling tired so you become irritable
- Time of day – after dinner you eat dessert
- Presence of a person – your response may be to become angry with them
- Work Deadline – so you procrastinate.

Rewards often appear in the brain as 'feel good' chemicals such as dopamine or oxytocin. As you repeat behaviour, the brain starts to become addicted. We are wired to reduce pain or discomfort, that's why habits are often destructive. You put off 'pain' and hand it over to your future self through procrastination; or, you may avoid dealing with something or someone by drinking alcohol. While some habits may make us feel better in the short term, they're often inherently destructive, that's why it's so important to review our way of 'being'. We often live in reaction to our internal dialogue, however this doesn't have to be the case.

Your current decision making is governed by two key factors:

1. Your unconscious brain – which is fed by your past habits and rewards
2. Your conscious brain – that is fuelled by future goal achievement and rewards

It's difficult to move forwards when you are being pulled in both directions!

EXERCISE

On a scale from one to ten, where would you rate your life in the following areas?

- *Health*
- *Wealth*
- *Relationships*
- *Business / Career*

It doesn't actually matter whether you rated high or low, what matters are the decisions you make from this point forward in getting to where you want to be.

Our results are what they are because we are genetically wired to save energy and to stay in our comfort zones. While you can't erase your old habits, you can replace them with more productive ones. Vital to success is to be mindful of how you are 'being'.

Creating new habits takes effort initially. As you repeat the process it will become easier as you instil a new benchmark. The key is to interrupt the current pattern. Look at the trigger (whether that be internal or external) and create a 'switch':

- If you want junk food, drink a glass of water
- If you feel angry, go for a walk
- If you think you need alcohol, call a friend

- If you want retail therapy, donate the money to charity instead

If you want to add more positive habits, visual cues can be helpful:

- Put floss next to your toothbrush
- Set your gym clothes out the night before, ready for the morning
- Put photos of your family on your desk to inspire you to stay on track throughout your day

Then you have the basics: if you tend to feel like junk food while you're watching TV, don't buy it. Our environment has a huge impact on our behaviour and our mindset. If we know that a bag of chips is sitting in the cupboard, then we'll probably eat them – out of habit! If they're not there, we're more likely to eat a healthier choice if that's all that's available.

Installing a new habit is like all types of goal setting – *you need a structure.*

SETTING GOALS TO WIN

One of the main reasons why goals are not achieved is that setting goals happens in the conscious part of the brain and achieving goals occurs in the subconscious brain (which is all about your habits and beliefs). If you haven't recognised and removed your destructive stories and fears (as outlined above), you will encounter resistance or sabotage as your conscious and unconscious parts of the brain collide.

TEN TIPS FOR ACHIEVING YOUR GOALS:

1. What is the vision for you and your life? Is your goal compatible?
2. What is your 'why' for achieving your goal? You need an emotional connection that will get you out of bed in the morning even when you don't feel like it.

3. If you want different results, you need to extend yourself. When you do this, you step up a level and that becomes the new norm. The results you're experiencing today are due to staying within the parameters of your comfort zone.

4. Create specific written goals. This gives your brain clarity and creates a vision for when you arrive at your destination.

5. "Are you interested or committed?" Alan Brown's quote is very poignant to achieving goals. Interested people make excuses, those that are committed are accountable. If you find that you're not that interested in a goal, either reframe it so that you're committed, or choose another goal.

6. Clear deadlines: what you need to do by when; and when the result will be seen.

7. Strategies for completion: Setting a goal and taking action to complete it happens in two different parts of the brain. To assist in creating harmony between the two, write down three strategies as to how you can achieve the goal. Also include the behaviour required to support you on your journey.

8. Recognise resistance. Do you have a fear or a story that's holding you back? Visualisation can help. The brain doesn't know the difference between an image in your imagination and reality (that's why we get what we focus on). By seeing and feeling what it's like to achieve your goal, you bring normalisation to the conscious and subconscious parts of the brain. When you achieve this, resistance will naturally dissipate.

9. Enrol an accountability partner or coach to keep you on track. Sportspeople do it, and it's just as important to have someone by your side in life.

10. Practice and refine. If you fail, don't judge yourself; keep trying. Practice and persistence is the key to success.

We cannot solve our problems with the same thinking we used when we created them.
~ Albert Einstein

We all have the same amount of time in the day. The difference between those who achieve their goals and those who don't is a matter of priorities, many of which can be attributed to positive mindset, beliefs, habits and goal setting. We hear about 'overnight' success stories and want the same for ourselves. We don't consider the details of how they arrived there in the first place, or that their 'overnight' success required planning and discipline – and actually took years in the making. If you want different results for you and your life you need different choices and another way of 'being'. Instead of attaching yourself to an outcome, take the time to build a foundation of success to work with into the future.

So, how long will this process take? Unfortunately, changing habits and achieving goals doesn't come with a magic formula, it's different for everyone. The key is to take action and implement the strategies above. People often consume energy looking for the magic ingredient to their lives, but they never take action; expecting results to magically appear.

Change does not come from just gathering knowledge, for without implementation, we continue to think the same things, feel the same things and do the same things over again.

So, what about you, are you an action taker?

About Stephanie

Stephanie Caldow grew up on a farm in rural Australia. In her late teens she suffered from chronic pain (due to a degenerative spinal condition), and concerns about her mental health. Determined not to be constrained by these obstacles, she began a quest to understand how mental, social and environmental factors impact our health, mindset and results. She travelled solo through Africa at age 19, has hiked mountains on six continents (including Mount Everest base camp), and ran the Great Wall of China Marathon. She attributes her resilience, relentless curiosity, creative thinking and pragmatic approach to those earlier physical and mental challenges, and her founding years on the farm.

For the last 20 years, Stephanie has run a number of successful businesses, and undertaken studies in a range of subjects including positive psychology, conversational intelligence, leadership and performance. She has worked with companies (ranging from 4 to 1000+ employees) in Indonesia, Canada, the UK, Dubai, New Zealand and Australia.

As Director of Think Collective, her goal is to "inspire the world to think differently, to live fearlessly, and to experience what it is to put forth their best". She now shares this with individuals, small business and corporations as a Consultant, Leadership Coach and Success Mentor.

Amongst other things, Stephanie is currently working on a book about love and loss, *FLOURISHING AFTER HEARTACHE*. She lives with her husband in Melbourne, Australia.

If you would like to learn more about how mental, social and environmental factors impact your results, and those of your business, you can contact us at:

- Email: thinkcollective@outlook.com
- Website: www.thinkcollective.com.au

CHAPTER 19

HOW TO SUCCESSFULLY DRIVE CHANGE IN YOUR ORGANIZATION

BY EZEQUIEL TEROL

Have you ever found yourself wondering why it is difficult to get people in your organization to accept the changes you decided to make, for the best of the whole group? Enrique does.

He runs the subsidiary of a multinational in Spain. During our first 45-minute discovery session, we started talking generalities about his successful business: how he was consistently achieving the double-digit growth his headquarters required from him, every year for the last three years. He explained to me how he, as a leader, deeply cared about developing his people through regular training over the years (both on technical skills and on soft skills). He even told me he had replaced his HR Director because the previous one didn't have that sense of servant leadership. He also placed a fair amount of pride in explaining to me how he had brought with him a part of his team from the previous company he had worked for. In fact, 20% of his current staff had followed him through two company changes. This had created a sense of team belonging. Everything seemed rolling perfectly well.

…Until I asked him about the challenges he was foreseeing over the next 12 months, which he felt his team was not ready to tackle. After making clear that everyone on his team was very capable and well prepared, he moved in his chair, put his forearms on the table, leaning towards me and told me: *"I have two sets of people in my organisation: the first is, the group I brought with me. They trust me in the direction I want to give, and when I ask, they execute. Sometimes, even if they don't get the whole picture, they tell me, "If you see it, it must be so." But the other group of people mostly don't get it. I even have an example of someone who complained when I asked him to embrace a new role with more responsibilities, because he was feeling demoted! He was indeed going to manage a smaller team with only 25% of the people he used to manage until then, but he was going to own and drive a range of activities with much higher value added for the company, rather than just approving vacations for more employees!"*

When I told him that **people don't resist change, but rather they resist being changed**, he said: *"I know that. But this is not the concern. I know exactly where I want the company to be in 18 months from now, and I have already made the decisions on my own. However, some people don't trust my viewpoint and don't want to act just on faith; they request explanations again and again. And while I invest as much time as needed with a junior person, I am not ready to do this kind of repetitive explanation with the people on my leadership team. The problem is that I need those people. And when they execute, they are good and efficient soldiers, they obtain great results."*

When I mentioned that different personality styles have different needs on how we communicate information in order to feel stimulated by a project, his answer was: *"I am of the opinion that all of us are better off working on our strengths, rather than on our weaknesses. Personally, I am not good at adapting to other people's communication styles, and frankly I don't see myself starting now. They are on my leadership team, they should be able to get it quickly or trust my approach."*

Sounds familiar? Enrique's frustration is understandable. He would like his team members to accept his views of the business, his vision for the company, buy into it, adhere and go execute. However, there are several realities that are getting in the way of this happening.

These are the seven things for you to consider when wanting to successfully drive change in an organization:

1. **Develop the 'Know – Like – Trust' factors.**
   Do the people in the organization see you as the leader to drive that change? As John C. Maxwell explains on his "21 Irrefutable Laws of Leadership", *"Leadership is influence, nothing more, nothing less."* In order for change to happen, you must develop your influence over the team or the organization you want to transform. So, the first question you need to ask yourself is, *"What perception does the organization have of me?"* If you're already perceived as the leader who can drive change, then you can work the next steps. If you realize that you don't have the required level of support and followers within the group that you want to help navigate change, you will have to first develop your influence. Ideally, you may want to identify the top influencers in the group and connect with them, so they become allies and sponsors of the change process, helping to get the rest of the group on board. *Key influencers in the group should know you, like you and trust you.*

2. **People can't hear until they've been heard: Understand your organization's relevant idea.**
   When defining the strategy for an organization, the process of casting a vision should include a collective contribution. As leaders, getting your dream team to draft their own individual visions and sharing them with you brings you invaluable insight, thanks to the diversity of views that

can enrich or challenge yours. While many people on the team may expect guidance and direction from you, don't underestimate the cohesion and adherence to the project that a collective vision casting may bring; it will allow the people in your team to feel they've been heard and to fully support the vision to be implemented—exactly the aspects that Enrique was missing from part of his leadership team. A collective vision-casting process may need an external, neutral facilitator. An experienced coach will help get all voices heard and help you develop an atmosphere of goodwill through the process. The collective vision casting allows you, as a second step, to ask every team member:

(i) to define which structural changes are required (if any) in their areas of expertise, to move in the direction you want to move, and

(ii) to draft their plans for how they expect to execute and implement the changes within their own environment.

Those draft plans will help you create the global plan and your business case, if a higher level sponsoring (investors, Board of Directors, senior management) is required for your ambition.

You will also be able to refer to the common vision when moments of difficulty, doubt and questioning may appear during the process of change.

3. **Get their buy-in: Communicate changes in a carefully worded way for everyone to feel energized.**
Be aware that different people have different personality profiles, and therefore, their working, collaboration, behavioural and communication styles may differ. This is not based on nationalities, cultural backgrounds or other common traits that could allow us to group people geographically. This is really an individual attribute. You can get to know your teams and their preferences better

in terms of communication, management, change, etc., by using the DISC model, developed and published by William Marston in 1928. It stands for Dominance-Influence-Stability-Compliance, the four personality factors. Each of those is present in every person, in different measures. And all combinations of the four factors have their strengths and their blind spots to be aware of.

By knowing yourself and the others around you in terms of your behavioural styles and communication preferences, it is easier to avoid the tension, the frustration and the conflicts, like the ones Enrique was experiencing. And therefore, collaboration, effectiveness and productivity are multiplied. The model can be used to work individual behaviour and communication as well as team dynamics.

Finally, different profiles react differently to change. The way you communicate such changes will be crucial to get the buy-in, support and the best out of your dream team through effectively connecting with them. If you have "high-S" (Stability) profiles in your team, those are the ones you want to get to adhere first to the change process. They are the more change-averse group, but because they seek the harmony of the team, once they are onboard, they will, in return, naturally convince the rest of the group to go your way.

When designing your communication strategy at this point, don't forget to infuse a feeling of haste. The change is necessary and cannot wait. It is important to transfer this feeling to the entire organization.

4. **Transform and grow your organization: Develop a culture of change and growth.**
Change is inevitable, growth is a choice. Everything changes, with different frequencies. From the solid buildings, changing at a very low frequency, to the stock

markets values, changing every second. There are two types of change: cyclical and structural. When you see cyclical change going south, you can bet that structural change is coming. As my friend Paul Martinelli likes to say, *"I don't know which industry or market you are in, but if you're running your business the same way you were five years ago, you better get ready to go out of business."*

Embracing change is a necessary means to navigate market conditions (and even drive new ones). While it can feel uncomfortable, it is a requirement for survival. So, you better get comfortable with being uncomfortable. And so do your teams. But embracing change is not enough. Getting insight from those situations requires being intentional. This is what will define the growth your organization members experience. How do you develop such a culture of change and growth? The *Law of Intentionality* says: *"Growth doesn't just happen."* A plan is required for it. Assuming our team will automatically grow just from experience, is one of those gap traps John C. Maxwell describes as preventing us from growing effectively. While experience will happen, gaining insights and learning from those experiences is an option.

Get your team to take time to reflect and build on their experiences (positive and negative) on a regular basis. Many leaders use the "Mess-up meetings" strategy: every team member is obligated to come with her or his failures, so everyone can learn from them and they lose negative power on the group morale. By combining planned growth with attitude, you become ready to take action when the opportunity appears. As a result, you create your own luck.

Finally, allow for flexibility in the process when things go wrong (they will), and adopt a learning attitude. There will be situations that will cause certain changes in direction. They must be handled, communicated and accepted as part of the success cycle: test, fail, learn, improve, re-enter, so they do not generate feelings of failure.

5. Build your army of change leaders: Value and leverage diversity.

Working in cross-cultural, cross-functional groups allows us to get complementary points of view on the different subjects treated. Whether you are working at headquarters and need to drive work in the field, or you need to drive a joint project with a different subsidiary, or even if your team is spread across five continents, you will get great value from leveraging diversity. Don't neglect getting first-hand information from a variety of people. While you may hold the last word on the strategy to follow, like Enrique does in our example above, everyone may bring different sensibilities and perspectives. As Simon Sinek says, *"Even the worst ideas have something you can build on."*

Listening to locals when trying to drive an initiative in a region or country you are not familiar with, may help avoid failures caused by cultural gaps, for example. Displaying a respectful, listening attitude will carry you very far in developing your leadership with diverse groups. This also means refraining from giving your opinions first! When running a meeting where you require others to contribute their views, practice the habit of listening to everyone first, and then be the last one to lay your cards on the table. This will give permission to everyone to express themselves without constraint, while allowing you to consider your team members' views and potentially adapt your contribution.

6. Look for low hanging fruits to create momentum.

"Momentum is a leader's best friend", to quote my mentor John C. Maxwell. It amplifies the positives and reduces the negatives. When wanting to implement a change within your organisation, getting to produce early results, even in small areas, has the effect of generating momentum in your favour. Your teams realize "it is feasible", and with those first

materializations, faith in the whole process gets reinforced. It is important therefore, to design a communication strategy that encompasses those successes, both internally and externally.

Internally, celebrating the first wins will make your employees feel involved and relate more to the change. Externally, getting the market to acknowledge your early efforts and successes can be even more reinvigorating for your teams. *Feed their faith, starve their fears.* Momentum will help you sustain the effort over the period of time required to implement the change process So, make sure the KPIs (Key Performance Indicators) you use to measure the success of your change processes are designed to allow those low-hanging fruits to score in favour of the initiative you are sponsoring.

7. **Make your changes last by anchoring new methods into the culture.**
   Driving lasting, positive change is what I strive to help my clients do. This is a crucial part of the change process, as it will require long term commitment and relentless display of the right attitudes and values by the leadership of the organisation. Start by rewarding the right behaviours, building upon the low-hanging fruits and lighthouse wins your team has produced. Follow by *"being the change you want to see in the world,"* as Gandhi said. Display the behaviours which reflect the values and the culture you expect your teams to live. *"People do what people see,"* it is the *Law of the Picture.*

   If your organization has a clearly defined *why*, link your new methods, products or services into the *golden circle* of your organization as *hows* or *whats* for the *why*. Discovering the *why* of your organization can be done with the help of an external facilitator, based on the body of work by Simon Sinek. It has helped numerous organizations successfully navigate periods of identity crisis and come out of the tunnel with renewed purpose, clarity and success.

Successfully driving change within an organization, with positive and lasting results, is an art. It requires preparation, intentionality and long-term commitment as a leader. Servant leadership will help you navigate the situations that arise and build the teams you need for sustained growth. I trust the application of these seven principles will help you drive change processes with your organization in the future.

I have helped leaders implement these principles to change company cultures, build new teams and accelerate business growth. And I have witnessed amazing results as the leaders grew in the process as much as their teams. This was the case for Enrique, who managed to regain his leadership team's support, dramatically improve the communication across his organisation and blow-up his fiscal year targets. As with my good wishes for Enrique, I wish you the brilliant success you deserve.

About Ezequiel

Ezequiel Terol is an optimist who strives to help others discover a better version of themselves, so that together we can create a more human world.

With a strong 20-year career in the corporate world, Ezequiel sharpens his leadership skills developing businesses for companies such as Orange, Nortel Networks, Microsoft and Oracle, with teams and projects spanning across Europe, the Middle East, Africa, the Americas and Asia. Collaboration, out-of-the-box thinking, competitivity and passion for transmission have been his most valuable tools, devoted to the continuous success of his clients.

Today, Ezequiel serves and inspires leaders in organizations of different sizes. He helps them implement positive, lasting changes, in order to create environments where their teams develop their full potential. Ezequiel trains, coaches and speaks internationally, specializing in a humanistic approach for servant leadership and change management, leveraging tools like NLP and DISC.

To maximize the impact he can have with his clients in the areas of leadership, communication and team effectiveness, Ezequiel has established partnerships with John C. Maxwell (he is an Executive Director within *The John Maxwell Team* and the President of *The John Maxwell Team France*), Marshall Goldsmith (he is an Associate Coach with the *Marshall Goldsmith Stakeholder Centered Coaching*[1] organization) and TTI Success Insights®, the leader of online evaluation tools. Ezequiel is also the founder and director of his coaching academy in Spain, based on the Concept-Therapy® works developed by Dr. Thurman Fleet. Through his *Coaching and Leadership Academy*, Ezequiel helps individuals develop their skills and reach their goals.

Under his brand *Lead 2 Multiply*, Ezequiel supports leaders and their teams, refining their strategic thinking process and the definition and implementation of their development and growth plans.

In addition to his for-profit activity, Ezequiel also collaborates with John

---

1. The Stakeholder Centered Coaching is a measured leadership growth process, where results are guaranteed (no growth, no fees).

Maxwell and his Leadership Foundation in pro-bono programs, bringing Transformational Leadership to developing countries, and training the youth in France and Spain on values. (*Global Youth Initiative*).

He questions individuals and organizations that he believes he can help as follows:
- Do you have a strategic project for which your team doesn't feel well-equipped?
- Do you foresee challenges to face or opportunities to leverage in the coming months and don't feel right now like you and your organization will maximize your impact?
- Do you wish to discover the *why* of your organization or to improve the leadership, communication, collaboration and effectiveness within your team?

He states unequivocally that, *"You do have a phenomenal potential... let's talk and put all chances on your side to make the mark on this world you deserve and were born to make!"*

Contact information for Ezequiel:
- Telephone: +33 6 70 61 10 71
- Email: ezequiel@lead2multiply.com
- LinkedIn: https://www.linkedin.com/in/ezequielterolrivas/

CHAPTER 20

HOW TO SELL YOUR BUSINESS FOR MORE THAN IT'S WORTH

BY JIM BENO

According to Best Selling author Paul Forsberg in his book, *The 5 Fundamental Elements of Every Successful and Sellable Business:* "You could take any 100 businesses and put them up for sale as they currently operate, and 80 out of 100 will never be sold." One of the best places you can advertise your business for sale is *BizBuySell.com*. At any given time, *BizBuySell* will have 45,000 + businesses for sale. *BizBuySell* produces a *Quarterly Insight Report* that analyzes sales and listing prices of small businesses across the United States.

According to their *Quarterly Insight Reports*, over the last 18 quarters, on average about 2,000 of those businesses listed are sold per quarter – that is about 5% of the businesses listed per quarter. Why is this number so low? Because most businesses are overpriced compared to the cash flow the business generates and the risk associated with that cash flow. A business sale price is normally equal to the business cash flow (owner benefits) times a multiple. With the exception of a strategic purchase, the multiple is determined by the risk the buyer perceives. Think of the equation: SP = C x M (Selling Price = Cash Flow x Multiple). The multiple (M) is determined by the risk of the acquisition, the higher the risk the smaller the multiple.

If you want to sell your business for more than it's worth you need to increase the value by increasing your cash flow and/or decreasing the Buyer's risk.

BELOW ARE 7 ACTION STEPS TO INCREASE YOUR BUSINESS VALUE

1) **Increase your revenue and cash flow:**
   A higher cash flow equals a higher business value. Buyers also consider the business purchase less risky when revenues and profits are increasing year-over-year. To a buyer, growing revenues equals growth potential which lowers a buyer's risk. Selling a business where the revenues and profits have been declining year-over-year is not only a difficult sale, but will always lead to a smaller multiple of cash flow. Buyers are skeptical when they see declining sales and profits and assume the Seller is looking to unload the business, regardless of the Seller's true reason for selling. When you are thinking of selling, focus on increasing revenues and profits and this will greatly increase your sales price. This has a 2x effect on your selling price (SP), because it increases both the C and M in the formula: SP = C x M.

2) **Reduce the business dependency on you (the owner):**
   How would your business perform if you were absent for an extended period of time? The more dependent your business is on you, the harder it will be to sell and the more risk it will be for the buyer. Businesses that are dependent on the owner(s) and where all the customers know the owner personally are much harder to sell and tend to sell for a smaller multiple. If you want to sell your business for a higher multiple, make your business less dependent on you! Make sure your customers are customers of the business

and not customers of yours! To illustrate, I will discuss two companies I recently sold.

The first company sold for $2.6 million dollars, which was the full asking price of the business. The owner received 90% of the sale price at closing and he financed 10% of the sale over a few years. The business went under contract within 45 days from when our ads went live and the business closed in about 90 days from when our ads went live. In this particular business, the owner had very limited interaction with the customers. All the staff, who would be staying with the new owner, handled daily activities. The owner managed key personnel and handled accounting duties. Accounting duties are easily outsourced, thus the business was able to sell very quickly and for the full asking price.

The second business was listed for $1.2 million. The cash flow was $430,000 and growing. The business was fairly priced at $1.2 million, based on the cash flow and growth of the business. Dozens of buyers considered this business, yet it took 16 months to go under contract and about 18 months to close. Two different brokers before I took the listing tried to sell this business but could not. The challenge was that the sales person was the owner. The business ultimately sold for $1 million, (17% discount) and the owner received about 65% of the sale price at closing and the remainder of the 35% was set up as owner financing and an earn-out. If the owner would have had one sales person in place that would have stayed with the business, I believe this business would have sold for close to the asking price and the owner would have received more money upfront.

3) <u>Reduce business dependency on large customers:</u>
Ideally, no customer will make up more than 15% of your revenue. Sometimes you land a large client, which is great for business. However, if 90% of your revenue is coming from 5 or 6 customers, this is a riskier purchase for a buyer and

will make it harder to sell the business and have a negative impact on the multiple you receive for your business.

4) Reduce the business dependency on any key employee or key supplier:

Sometimes owners rely heavily on long-term employees. Their knowledge and experience is vital to operating the business. Because of this, it is important to have proper documentation on how each job is performed. Cross training employees can also minimize dependence on any one employee and reduce a buyer's risk, thus increasing the selling multiple. Likewise, it is a good idea not to rely on one or two suppliers. Getting occasional price quotes from your supplier's competitors can not only reduce your COGS but can lower a Buyer's risk.

5) Reduce the amount of working capital it takes to run your business:

When a buyer considers purchasing your business, beyond the purchase price consideration is the amount of money or working capital it takes to run the day-to-day operations. A business that requires a large amount of working capital to run has more risk to a buyer and with everything else being equal, will sell for a lower multiple. If you can receive payment for your goods or services before or at the time of the transaction, this will lower the working capital required to run your business.

6) Increase the amount of recurring revenue your business has:

The higher the percentage of your revenue that is recurring, the less risky the acquisition will be for a buyer. The majority revenue from a fitness center comes from a monthly draft on the first of the month. If a buyer was looking to acquire a fitness center that had monthly operating expenses of $600,000 and average monthly revenue of $900,000, with everything else being equal, the higher the monthly draft, the more value the business has. If you want to lower a buyer's risk and increase your value, make more of your revenue recurring.

7) **<u>Increase the ratings of your online reviews:</u>**
Any buyer thinking about purchasing your business will research your company online and will read all the online reviews they can find on your business. Today, ratings on Google, Yelp and other rating sites can have both a positive or negative impact on your business. After a positive experience from your customers, encourage them to go online and leave your business a positive review. In today's environment, it is very easy for a buyer or potential new customer to see your company's track record on customer satisfaction. Good ratings lead to more customers and make a buyer feel good. Bad online ratings will make a buyer perceive the purchase as risky. Unfortunately, most customers only take the time to rate a business if they are upset; this is why you need to ask happy customers to rate you online.

Increasing the value of your business is the first step in "selling your business for more than it's worth". The second step is you must market it confidentially to the masses and also know how to handle buyers when they inquire about your business. While marketing your business to the masses seems obvious, I am surprised on how many times it is overlooked! How can you sell your business for more than it's worth if only a few people know it's for sale? I am astonished when a business owner, who has worked hard to build a million dollar business, doesn't spend a few thousand dollars to confidentially market their business for sale. The more places you advertise your business, the more buyers you will have inquiring. Normally, more buyers will lead to a higher selling price. Do not be afraid to spend money advertising your business! *You have to confidentially get the word out to the masses if you want to sell your business for more than it's worth!*

Besides reducing a buyer's risk and advertising your business to the masses, you should understand all the major steps that take place in the sale of a business. I could write an entire book on this topic so below is a very brief outline.

HERE ARE 11 STEPS MOST PROFESSIONAL BROKERS WILL PERFORM WHEN SELLING A BUSINESS

1) <u>Determine your cash flow or Seller's Discretionary Earnings (SDE):</u> All buyers will want to see the cash flow of your business as it is the reason they are buying your business.

2) <u>Review a comparison report for similar businesses that sold:</u> A comp. report will tell you what similar businesses sold for and will give you an idea where your business should be priced. You should be able to purchase a comp. report for less than $300 if you are not using a broker.

3) <u>Determine your business selling price:</u> Your comparison data report will give you the number of similar businesses that sold along with the median, maximum and minimum multiple of SDE. You can ask an above average price for your business if you have reduced a buyer's risk by implementing items we discussed earlier. There are obviously a lot of other factors that go into determining an asking price, but this should give you a good idea on what a reasonable asking price is.

4) <u>Prepare your Confidential Marketing Booklet (CMB) to give to buyers:</u> Your CMB should discuss your sales and cash flow for the last few years and highlight business strengths and any selling points of your business. It might include the benefits of the location, industry information, growth potential and information on the competition. Tell the buyer all the reasons why your business is a great opportunity. You will also want to include pictures of the business, a financial worksheet that shows historical sales, expenses,

EBITDA and SDE. If possible include a term sheet from an SBA lender stating the business has been pre-qualified for an SBA loan.

5) <u>Create an ad that attracts buyers:</u> It is crucial that your ad is very generic. You do not want to disclose the name or address of your business in your ads. This information should only be disclosed to buyers who have completed a Non Disclosure Agreement (NDA). Your ad should only discuss the strengths of the business. The most important part of the ad is the headline. You have only a few words to get the buyer's attention!

6) <u>Advertise your business:</u> There are hundreds of places you can advertise your business. You will get the best global exposure and 'bang for your buck' by advertising your business on the internet. There is no shortage of business-for-sale websites online. Plan on paying about $200 - $600 per ad, depending on what options you choose and how long your ad runs. I recommend running your ad for at least 6 months.

7) <u>Pre-screen your prospective buyers:</u> After you receive a call or email about your business, request that the potential buyer completes a Non-Disclosure Agreement (NDA) before discussing any confidential information (business name, location, etc.). We strongly recommend all legal documents you use are reviewed by a local attorney. Laws vary from state to state.

8) <u>Address buyer questions and prepare for buyer meetings:</u> After a buyer has completed your NDA and you have sent out your marketing booklet, it is time to follow up. Call the buyer to see what questions they have. Every buyer will ask why you are selling. If you are under 55 years old, you really need to consider your answer.

9) <u>Request a Letter of Intent (LOI):</u> The Letter of Intent (LOI) will come from the buyer or the buyer's attorney. The purpose of the LOI is to formally make an offer on your business. It will spell out most of the major terms of the offer such as price, any financing requested, length of time you are expected to stay on for training and other crucial items in the offer. The presenting of the LOI is the start of the negotiating process. If you do not already have legal counsel, I highly recommend that you retain local legal counsel before responding to an LOI.

10) <u>Work with your CPA and Attorney during due diligence:</u> Over half of all deals come apart during the due diligence. During the due diligence period, your buyer will request information that is very confidential. It is crucial that all the information you supply is congruent. Before you start releasing the confidential information in the due diligence process, your attorney may advise you to have a more detailed Non-Disclosure and Non-Compete or Non-Solicit Agreement signed. *Discuss with your counsel!* The best way to conduct the due diligence is to upload all the requested documents in a secured data room. You don't want to have all of your confidential information in an unsecured site or in paper format where you can't control who is reviewing your confidential information.

You should consult with your CPA *before* the APA is drafted up. I recommend discussing the tax implications of the sale with your CPA before you even negotiate terms of the sale. Every Seller's situation will be different which is why you need to discuss tax implications of your sale with your personal CPA. *Many times, your CPA can save you tens of thousands if not hundreds of thousands of dollars in unnecessary taxes.*

11) <u>Close the Deal and get paid:</u> Once the Asset Purchase Agreement (APA) is agreed upon and the Buyer is satisfied with the entire due diligence documents you provided, you are ready to set up the closing. All the work is done, and it is time to collect your money. Closing requirements will vary from state to state; your attorney will guide you through the process. If you didn't sleep the night before, that is normal.

Congratulations, you can now relax!

[Business Broker Experts, Inc. and Jim Beno are not providing legal or tax advice. When selling your company, Business Broker Experts, Inc. and Jim Beno highly recommend you work with local legal counsel and a CPA.]

About Jim

Jim Beno is the CEO of Business Broker Experts, Inc. Jim received a bachelor's degree in Accounting and also has an MBA. Jim has also achieved a CBI (Certified Business Intermediary) designation in which less than 10% of all business brokers have achieved. Jim has owned, operated and sold his own businesses so he understands all the challenges a business owner faces. Jim has been working with and consulting with business owners since 2003. Jim has sold businesses and has strategized with CEO's of all different sized companies from just a few employees to companies with over 50 employees.

Jim's extensive background in business coupled with his conversations with thousands of different business owners and potential buyers helped Jim get selected to write this chapter on "How to sell your business for more than it's worth." Jim is also an active member in the following organizations:

- M&A Source
- International Business Brokers Association (IBBA)
- Midwest Business Brokers and Intermediaries (MBBI)

Jim's company offers full service brokering for businesses owners ready to sell today, and the company offers Exit planning and consultation for business owners looking to sell in the next 2-5 years.

Jim states that: "I am honored that I was selected to write this chapter on, 'How to sell your business for more than it's worth.' I would like to thank Brian and his staff as they were very professional and wonderful to work with."

Jim can be reached at:

- jimbeno@businessbrokerexpertsinc.com
- Office: 800-708-7605.

[Business Broker Experts, Inc. and Jim Beno are not providing legal or tax advice. When selling your company, Business Broker Experts, Inc. and Jim Beno highly recommend you work with local legal counsel and a CPA.]

CHAPTER 21

THE WILL TO SMILE AGAIN...YOU HAVE OPTIONS!

BY DR. JOSEPH MOUSSA

Early in my dental career, my dad had periodontal disease. The only way I could help him was to send him to a periodontist. I was always heartbroken when he would come back from his gum surgery in extreme pain and discomfort. This is because the traditional treatment for gum disease involves cutting into the gum tissue, folding it back, and then manually cleaning the teeth to remove plaque and tartar accumulations below the gum line. It was invasive and extremely painful for him.

Back then I had heard of a new procedure called LANAP. LANAP stands for Laser Assisted New Attachment Procedure. It is a minimally invasive, healthier approach to treat gum disease, using a laser instead of a scalpel. I was intrigued by the description of what it did and how it was helping patients. It's basically a, "No cut...No sew," approach to getting rid of diseased tissue from the gums and encourages the gums to reattach to the teeth.

I knew I had to investigate it further. After learning more, I got the LANAP training and performed it on half of my dad's mouth. Six months later he went back to his periodontist. They were amazed at how good my dad's gums were on that side. Ever since then, I have been passionate about helping my patients with this treatment. I was one of the first dentists in the state of New Jersey to adopt it and have helped over 400 of my patients with this less invasive treatment.

Now, there are several things you should be aware of when it comes to your gum health.

1) Gum disease is all too common, affecting nearly 50% of all American adults. Bacteria and plaques continually accumulate on the surface of the teeth. Tender gum tissue can become inflamed when exposed to germs, and it begins to pull away from the tooth, creating a pocket between your tooth and gum tissue.

2) Gum disease makes your gingiva tender, swollen, and red; gingivitis may advance into periodontitis, which may make cause severe infections, and eventually leads to tooth loss if left untreated.

3) The traditional cure for gum disease involves clipping the gum tissue, folding it back, and after that manually cleaning the tooth to remove tartar and plaque accumulations beneath the gum line.

But LANAP, which stands for Laser Assisted New Attachment Procedure, is a newer, more successful, and a whole lot more comfortable remedy to eradicate the diseased tissue and also encourage the gingiva to reattach to the teeth.

Here are some Frequently Asked Questions on LANAP

i. What is LANAP?

The FDA-cleared laser treatment is also known as LANAP. It provides a less debilitating treatment than conventional periodontal surgery. If you're seeking a professional providing LANAP, then it's necessary to not only search for one with authenticity, but to find one with experience.

LANAP is the only proven research method leading to true periodontal regeneration. It permits for new bone growth and attachment of the gum to the teeth.

ii. What's the LANAP protocol?

The LANAP protocol is a minimally invasive gum disease therapy that employs a particular dental laser, the PerioLase® MVP-7™. The LANAP protocol is the first and only protocol to receive FDA clearance for Authentic Regeneration, which is new growth of cementum, new periodontal ligament, and a new alveolar bone. These three components are necessary for full function. The LANAP protocol has been in widespread use by the dental community for several years.

iii. What can I expect during LANAP therapy?

The LANAP protocol is performed at a dentist's office under local anesthesia. Before the procedure, the dentist does a periodontal charting and takes X-rays to make a correct diagnosis and determine the extent of the disease. A tiny laser fiber is inserted between the tooth and the gum, and the infection and diseases are cleared off without cutting the teeth. The roots of the teeth are then completely cleaned of plaque and tartar, and the laser can be used again with a different setting and make a secure, firm fibrin blood clot to seal the pocket.

The dentist treats 50% of the patient's mouth in every session, and many patients have the ability to drive themselves back to work or home following the procedure.

iv. Who will carry out the LANAP protocol that helps patients with gum disease?

Only LANAP trained dentists may perform the LANAP protocol.

v. What instruction does my LANAP trained doctor have?

All dentists certified to carry out the technique are needed to complete the comprehensive, clinical, hands-on, dentist-to-dentist training within the course of a year at the Institute for Advanced Laser Dentistry. This in-depth training ensures that physicians are skilled to carry out the LANAP protocol.

vi. How Long is the LANAP Treatment?

LANAP periodontal surgery is a full-mouth procedure usually completed in two, 2-hour visits.

You might be a candidate for LANAP if...

A. You Have Deep Gingival Pockets
The deeper your gingival pockets, the more advanced your case of periodontitis. Candidates for LANAP typically have a gingival pocket depth of at least 5 mm. If you have more shallow pockets, even less invasive procedures may be enough to halt the progression of periodontal disease.

B. You Exhibit Symptoms of Periodontal Disease
Patients who exhibit symptoms of any form of periodontal disease—mild or advanced—are candidates for LANAP. Here are some things that your LANAP certified dentist will look for during your initial exam:

- Gum Recession
- Loose Teeth
- Gums That Bleed Easily

If you do have periodontal disease, the doctor will work with you to plan your treatment. Patients are commonly asked to alter their standard oral hygiene practices to be more thorough or integrate an antibacterial mouthwash or rinse. Next, the dentist will talk with you about when you should have LANAP and what to expect during the procedure.

C. Recommendations from Other Dental Professionals
You might also be a candidate for LANAP if your normal doctor or dentist recommends you to a periodontist.

Four advantages of the LANAP protocol to the treatment of gum disease:

1. **Less post operative pain:** Employing the PerioLase MVP-7 dental laser, the LANAP protocol helps prevent cutting and stitching of the gums. Consequently, patients typically have a minimal post-operative discomfort.

2. **Faster recovery time:** Many patients have the ability to return to their routine daily activities instantly following the procedure, which normally requires less than a 24-hour recovery period. Following the traditional scalpel and suture operation, recovery may take up to a month, through which patients may undergo considerable pain and swelling.

3. **Healthy teeth with minimal recession:** Whenever your teeth are all cut, the tissue shrinks and may show more of your tooth origin. Since the LANAP protocol doesn't cut your teeth, the tissue stays intact.

4. **Regeneration without foreign material:** Since the PerioLase laser stimulates your body's own healing response, your LANAP dentist does not have to add foreign growth factors.

One more thing to know...

LANAP is The World's First Ever FDA Clearance for True Regeneration™!

No other laser periodontal therapy or laser device can claim True Regeneration including new bone formation. True Regeneration is a completely new and original FDA clearance based on completely new scientific evidence and performance data. Per the FDA, Periodontal regeneration true periodontal regeneration of the attachment apparatus (new cementum, new periodontal ligament, and new alveolar bone) on a previously diseased root surface when used specifically in the LANAP protocol.

GIVING THE WILL TO SMILE AGAIN

Here's what one of my patients said about his treatment:

"Dr. Moussa is probably the best dentist in New York and New Jersey. He's always up to date with the latest cutting-edge technologies and has all the most modern, state-of-the-art equipment. **By his recommendation, he performed the LANAP procedure on my gums in his office. He literally saved my teeth!** This procedure is hands down better than the old way (scalpel). Besides that, he's quite personable, gentle, and sensitive to your needs. You won't find a better dentist!! My highest recommendation!!!"

When I hear this from my patients, I feel joy inside. It is one of the greatest gifts I can give to them. Recently, I got my highest level LANAP Regenerative Specialist Certificate, because I want to keep up with modern technology and procedures that help my patients the best way I can. It has now been over 20 years of helping my patients get a healthy smile and I have loved every minute of it!

About Dr. Joseph

Joseph Moussa, DDS, FICOI and Owner of Montclair Dental Spa, in Montclair, New Jersey has been changing people's lives with his gum rejuvenation, implant dentistry and full reconstruction of smiles for over 20 years.

He originally graduated from Damascus University College of Dentistry; the oldest and most prestigious University of its kind in 1993. He served two years as a Lieutenant in the Army performing Dentistry in the clinics and hospitals. He then enjoyed a very successful practice abroad for seven years, but he felt as if something was missing. He fell in love with a branch of Dentistry that was up and coming. He craved to know more about these specific procedures.

He chose to leave his home to learn more about the exciting field of Implantology and Dentistry here in America. He was immediately accepted to the distinguished New York University Dental School to hone his skills and to satisfy his need to know more about implants and Cosmetic Dentistry. He graduated in May of 2003. His professors were so impressed with his skills and desire to learn, they offered him the position of Associate Professor of Implantology in the post-graduate program of New York University Dental School.

Dr. Moussa not only enjoys Implantology, he has dedicated many hours to training in one of the most prestigious programs on the east coast for Esthetic Dentistry. This training included porcelain veneers and full porcelain restorations. His training and desire to perform the best Dentistry possible, drives him to continue to stay involved with the University and to increase his dental knowledge with many continuing education courses.

Dr. Moussa stays on the cutting edge with the latest in high-tech equipment ranging from digital x-rays and lasers to digital crown impressions without the use of goopy impression material.

His passion for Dentistry and compassion for his patients proves to be a very successful combination. He maintains memberships in well-known academies such as: FICOI, International Congress of Oral Implantology, and the American Academy of Cosmetic Dentistry. He recently achieved his highest-level of certification as a LANAP Regenerative Specialist. Plus, he's been chosen as one of the Top Docs for New Jersey, three years in a row.

Also, his belief in a more natural approach to dentistry has lead him to become a well-known "Biological" Dentist in the state of New Jersey, being a member of The International Association of Mercury-Safe Dentists, The International Academy of Biological Dentistry and Medicine and The International Academy of Oral Medicine and Toxicology.

Dr. Moussa says:
"I treat everyone as if they were my family, whether they are an internationally known singing star, a grandchild of a famous person or someone who just walks into my office. Everyone deserves a beautiful smile. I want them all to have that. It is the least I can do to help change people's lives."

Contact information:

- Montclairdentalspa@gmail.com
- www.twitter.com/montclairds
- www.facebook.com/Montclairds

CHAPTER 22

HOW TO DEVELOP
THE WILL TO WIN

BY JIM CATHCART, CSP, CPAE

My friend Peter Vidmar, Olympic Champion, told me, *"As a gymnast, almost every day, my goal was to train about 15 more minutes than the rest of my teammates. That little extra focus over a few years led to some perfect 10's at the Olympic Games. Perfection does take time...(so) see what 15 (extra) minutes a day can do for you."*

THE WILL TO PREPARE

Most everyone has the *Desire* to win. Some even have the *Will* to win. But in order to actually win, they also must develop the will to *Prepare*. Boxer Muhammed Ali is famous for saying that his fights weren't just won in the ring. They were won in the training that he did in preparation for the bout. If he hadn't done the intense and painful training that was needed, then he'd have been unprepared to face his competition and would have lost.

My amazing mentor, Joe Willard, once had me grab his wrist and shake his arm while he held a cup of water. Of course, it spilled, and he then asked me, "Why did the water come out of the cup?" I replied, "Because I shook your arm." He said, "No, if you had shaken my arm as I held an empty cup then all your effort would have been for naught. It came out because it was in there in the first place." If you don't study, plan, practice and train then winning won't be "in you in the first place."

Winners learn to love training. My grandson, Jason, as a preteen once told me that he really enjoyed practicing piano. I asked what he meant, and he said that the experience of trying, failing, adjusting and succeeding was what he enjoyed. Wow! Most people tend to give up when the learning or the effort becomes difficult. I guess that's why today in his late teens, Jason can now play: keyboard, guitar, ukulele, and drums quite well. He's also a semi-pro magician and Cardistry expert. Every day he carries a deck of cards with him and practices the expert manipulation of the deck in one hand, then the other, then both. He amazes his friends and quickly connects with strangers who are attracted by the oohs and ahhs of his audience.

Any of us could learn the tricks that Jason performs, but to perform them in such a way that they amaze even skeptical adults, that requires the will to practice.

My "other" job, when I'm not speaking or writing, is playing guitar and singing professionally. My wife and I perform together and with musical friends about once a month, and I frequently perform on my own. When I practice my music I usually devote about an hour or more to performing the songs that I haven't done in a while. My music is the "oldies" from the 50s-60s-70s and there are 400 or more songs, so the ones that don't end up on my practice list also don't make it into my upcoming performances. I forgive myself for the mistakes I make in practice and I keep on playing until I get it right. But during a live performance any lack of practice and preparation would quickly show. What are the skills essential to your success that need a little brushing up?

1. Commit to the practice.
2. Set the dates and times.

3. Make an appointment with yourself and honor it just as you would an appointment with a prospective customer.

THE WILL TO WORK

My newest office employee was impressive in the interview and got along well with everyone. She was bright, articulate and appeared to be a great addition to our team...until. One day when she was given the day's checks to take them to the bank to be deposited (a part of her job assignment), she complained, "I'm not going in that direction when I leave the office and somebody else could do it just as easily." We let it go that day but when the pattern of whining repeated I let her go. She protested, of course, but I told her that if she wasn't willing to do the work then we didn't need her on the team.

My friend Marty, who is in his mid-eighties, is a member of my mountain hiking club. We meet three days a week at sunrise and hike or run 6 miles up and down the Santa Monica mountains near Los Angeles. Marty is always there, even when he doesn't feel like hiking. He even shows up a bit earlier than the rest of us because he doesn't hike as fast as he used to. Of the sixty people in our group of remarkable athletes and dedicated fitness addicts, Marty is the most admired. Why? Because he always shows up to do the work. He could make so many easy excuses and nobody would criticize him, but he doesn't. He may occasionally be still on the trail when the rest of us are on the return, but he still completes each hike without complaint.

What is "the work" for you? Do you show up early? Stay a bit late if needed? Complete each assignment fully? Do you read what you need to learn in order to do it well? It is not hard to find someone to do a job, but to find someone who will consistently do it well and without complaint, that is a treasure! My Dad drilled this into me early on. I remember when I would seek summer employment at the end of the school year. I'd often go to a business or industrial complex and just go door-to-door applying for menial labor positions until someone hired me. The work was hard and only paid minimum wage, which at that time was $1.25 an hour. (Yes, I'm aware how old that makes me seem.) But I always found a job! And once I got it, I'd show up early the next day, ready to work.

Don't just do "your" work, do THE work! Do what needs to be done to assure that your efforts will succeed.

THE WILL TO CHANGE

You didn't start out as you will need to be when you win. None of us did. We are not "eligible receivers" until we are down field in the open, and skilled and focused enough to catch the ball and score.

There are habits and mannerisms that we accumulate over the years and many of those don't serve us well. It could be a vocal pattern, or the use of certain vocabulary. It could be a work habit or a preferred way of doing something. It might even be our instinctive responses to what other people do, but somewhere in each of us there are traits that will get in our way when we strive to win.

J.C. Penney, the famous retailer, once said, "No one need live a minute longer as he (or she) is, because the Creator has endowed us with the ability to change ourselves."

Joe Willard, as a national leader in the insurance industry, once told me that he went from "eager new agent" to "agency sales leader" by asking one simple question every day: "How would the agency sales leader do what I'm about to do?" By using his more enlightened and successful future self as his role model he upgraded every action he took until it started producing successful results. He quickly became the agency's sales leader and then led his entire company. I adopted that question in my book, *The Acorn Principle*, and dubbed it "The Daily Question."

"How would the person I'd like to be do the things I'm about to do?" The more often you ask yourself this question, the more successful you will be.

THE WILL TO RESIST

Sales leader Mort Utley once told me that as a young sales person he followed his peers each morning to have breakfast together before beginning their sales activities. As he was departing the office he noticed that the company's top sales person was still in his office working. So, Mort invited him to join them for breakfast. To his surprise the agent gave Mort a handful of money and said, "I'll buy everyone's breakfast today, but I won't join you." Mort asked why and the agent said, "It is less expensive for me to stay here and make sales calls than it is for me to buy all of your breakfasts and to share a meal instead of doing the work." From that day forward Mort, too, stayed at work instead of doing "the popular thing" and following the crowd.

When I started jogging in order to lose weight and get fit (for the first time in my adult life), many of my friends discouraged me. They said, "Jogging isn't good for your knees. The repetitive motion and running on pavement will hurt your joints." I noticed that the people who were critical of my new chosen exercise were not personally fit nor committed to any useful regimen for getting fit. So, I went jogging.

It hurt. It hurt every time.

At first jogging was misery for me, but after a short time I became more fit and eventually dropped 52 lbs. of excess fat. Before long, I was able to run five miles nonstop and be happy as I ran. Today, 40 years later, I'm still fit with a 30" waist and I run six-mile mountain trails 3 days a week. There are always discouragers who will give you seemingly plausible reasons not to do what you've chosen to do. They say, "Don't work too hard" and "Take it easy", as if these were important cautions for us to heed. Not so, we need to learn to resist the naysayers and follow the path to our "win".

Diminish your time with negative people. Avoid TV shows, books and discussions that focus on people's weaknesses and cynicism. Resist the urges that tell you to quit. Do just one more step, one more call, one more minute of sustained effort. Resist the temptation to take the easy path. Nobody gets stronger by lifting the lighter weights. As my colleague Rory Vaden says, "Take the stairs!"

THE WILL TO PERSIST

Slow and steady wins the race, so says Aesop's fable of the tortoise and the hare. I don't know so much about the "slow," but I can assure you that "steady" dedication to stay the course and not let up on your effort, is indeed great advice.

As a young newlywed with no college degree and a low-paying job, I once heard Earl Nightingale, the Dean of Personal Motivation, on the radio, and I realized that I wanted to do what he was doing. I wanted to become a motivational speaker and author in order to help people grow and improve. But I had two conditions that would limit one's speaking and writing career: I had never given a speech, and I had nothing to say!

Still, I wanted more than anything to become a professional speaker and an expert in the field of human development. So, I committed to the discipline of spending at least one extra hour (beyond my work) in the study of human development. I became unreasonably dedicated to filling that hour or more each day with books, discussions with successful people, collaborating with fellow success seekers, or practice of the new techniques I'd been learning. I was fanatical about it. That means that I not only resisted the friends and family who were telling me to "lighten up" but I also refused to let a day pass without some new learning in it. Everywhere I went, I took along a recording or a book and filled each idle moment with some small amount of progress in my learning journey.

Within a year, others were noticing the "new me" and I was being sought for advice or to help someone else to improve themselves. Five years into my new path, I had left my menial job as a government clerk and become a full-time trainer and speaker. At first, I taught other people's courses and then, over time, I developed my own material and wrote my own training programs. Today, 40 years later, I have delivered over 3,100 paid presentations in all 50 United States and many foreign countries. I've served as president of the National Speakers Association, been inducted into the Sales & Marketing Hall of Fame and written 18 books published by the top publishers in the world. Who knew I could do that? I certainly didn't...yet. When I started this journey all I knew was what I wanted to do and that I was willing to do the work and stay the course until someday, finally, it would pay off.

You have the same opportunity, not in the same way necessarily, but you can change yourself, do the preparation, resist the skeptics, do the work and stay the course. You can literally change your world by following this process. And, if you truly commit to it, you may be able to change your company, your industry or the entire world. Every great thing that was ever done has begun with one individual who was unreasonably committed to making it happen. That can be you!

THE WILL TO WIN

This book is a treasure chest of great ideas, inspiring stories and clever strategies for winning. By learning from each different author, by re-reading each chapter at different times in your life and under different circumstances, you will have the "Eureka!" moments and gain the insights you'll need to overcome any obstacle. Not alone, not on first try, not in the ways that you might suspect, but succeed you will. There's that word again...

"Will." The people who attempt things say, "I'll try." The people who achieve things say, "I will!"

Will you?

About Jim

Jim Cathcart, CSP, CPAE is arguably the most award-winning professional speaker in the world. He has received: *The Golden Gavel Award* from Toastmasters International along with former recipients Tony Robbins, Zig Ziglar, Nido Qubein, Earl Nightingale and Walter Cronkite. He has also earned The Cavett Award and Speaker Hall of Fame award from the National Speakers Association. He's earned the Certified Speaking Professional designation and been inducted into the Sales & Marketing Hall of Fame in London. As former President of the National Speakers Association he has received the Lifetime Achievement Award and Distinguished Service Awards. He's also the cofounder of the China Speakers Association in Shanghai.

Mr. Cathcart was recently appointed as Entrepreneur in Residence to the Center for Entrepreneurship, School of Management at California Lutheran University. He has written and published 18 books including 3 international bestsellers: *Relationship Selling, The Acorn Principle* and *The Self-Motivation Handbook.* His latest book, in Mandarin & English, is *You Are The Speaker, 53 lessons on public speaking.*

Having delivered over 3,100 speeches and seminars around the world over the past 40 years, Jim has addressed groups from virtually every profession and industry. His TEDx video has received well over 1.25 million views, placing it in the top 1% of over 100,000 TED videos.

Despite all of his professional accomplishments, Jim Cathcart remains a down-to-earth regular guy. He's a life member of the American Motorcyclist Association, an avid mountain trail runner and a professional singer/guitarist who regularly performs at events and in clubs worldwide. His greatest strength lies in helping people discover how to use their natural abilities to succeed. He believes in: getting the job done, telling the truth, doing what is right and what works best, respecting all people and learning more every day of your life.

To receive an inspiring message once a week by email, connect with:

- acorn@aweber.com.

To check Jim's availability for speeches or interviews:

- Contact: info@cathcart.com
- Visit: www.Cathcart.com for over 730 pages of free resources, videos and more